Legends of Vancouver

E. Pauline Johnson (Tekahionwake)

A NEW EDITION
WITH AN INTRODUCTION
BY MARCUS VAN STEEN
AND ILLUSTRATED BY BEN LIM

McClelland & Stewart

Contents

E. Pauline Johnson

On a sunny summer day in the carefree Edwardian London of 1906, two visiting Canadians met and greeted each other, more warmly than even expatriates usually do because they both came from the proud but warm-hearted race of our first Canadians. The heavily-moustached, weather-beaten but dignified little man was Joe Capilano, a prominent chief of the Pacific Coast tribes, in London to appeal personally to the King regarding the alienation of Indian hunting lands. The stylishly-dressed lady with the warm brown eyes and the passionate mouth was Emily Pauline Johnson, who preferred to be called Tekahionwake, then riding easily on the first crest of her fame as a sweet Mohawk singer and vibrant entertainment personality. Out of this meeting grew a prized friendship, and the brief maturing of her literary powers which produced these *Legends of Vancouver*, her most lasting contribution to Canadian literature.

The stories in this volume, or most of them, are intimately connected with Vancouver and the hills and waters around it, but they are universal in their appeal, just as all great works of art are universal when they deal, as these stories do, with the sanctity of love; the desirability of faithfulness; the detestation of avarice; the admiration of strength and courage and kindliness, and the wish all parents feel to set an example of a clean life to their children. There are also hints of inherited folk memories —the Sea-Serpent story resembles the dragon tales of many races, and "The Deep Waters" is certainly the story of the flood that is found in many parts of the world.

None of these stories, as they appear here, can properly be classified as folklore. There is more in them of the sophisticated artistry of Pauline Johnson than of the simple imaginings of a primitive people. But the folklore is unmistakably there, lovingly embellished, almost transformed by the word skill of the Mohawk singer. One of the Legends Pauline did transpose into verse. Her "Ballad of Yaada," the last poem Pauline ever wrote, tells the same tale as "The Grey Archway." In at least one other case she had planned to retell one of the Legends. Among her papers after her death was found a sheet headed "The Ballad of Laloo" and the lines:

This is Laloo, chief of the tribe whose feet
Follow the murmuring Illecillewaet.

But that is all. The ballad of the story that appears here as "The Lost Island" was never written.

Emily Pauline Johnson was born on March 10, 1861, on the Six Nations Reservation at Brantford, Ontario. On her father's side she was of a noble Mohawk family, bearing a title that dates back to the days of Hiawatha and the fifty Indian leaders who formed the League of the Iroquois some half-century before Columbus crossed the Atlantic, and who are mentioned in the final sketch in this book, "A Royal Mohawk Chief." Her Indian name was Tekahionwake, the "Johnson" being a comparatively recent addition acquired from the great colonial leader, Sir William Johnson, who acted as godfather to Pauline's great-grandfather when he was baptized into the Christian faith at Niagara. Her grandfather, John Smoke Johnson, a hero of the War of 1812, married Helen Martin, a daughter of the great Mohawk chief George Martin and Catherine Rolleston, a white girl of German descent who had been carried off from a Pennsylvania settlement and brought up as an Indian. Their son, George Henry Martin Johnson, married Emily Susanna Howells of Bristol, the sister-in-law of the Anglican missionary on the Brantford Reservation. Miss Johnson, therefore, was more than half white, a fact that never kept her from proclaiming herself wholly Indian, as she was by law, by temperament, by choice, and by upbringing.

In one of her short stories Pauline tells how her mother, having defied her family to stand by the side of the young Mohawk chieftain who had won her heart, was determined that her four children "should be reared as Indians in spirit and in patriotism," loving the Indian legends, the Indian habits and customs, the Indian people. That her mother was successful is proved in every sentence of this book.

One of her many friends, the Canadian naturalist Ernest Thompson Seton, has recorded Miss Johnson as saying: "There are those who think they pay me a compliment in saying I am just like a white woman. I am Indian, and my aim, my joy, my pride, is to sing the glories of my people."

She also had little use for those who saw her talent coming from the Howells who had produced the novelist William Dean Howells. However, to compare Pauline with her famous cousin is like comparing a carefree, singing child with a bearded philosopher. W. D. Howells dissected life with thought and logic. Pauline experienced life, and sang for the same reasons that she laughed and wept. In her best work, her use of metaphor, her ability to express colour, light and shade, indicates that she owed much to her grandfather, Smoke Johnson, who was a famous orator known as "the Mohawk Warbler." In other words, as the critic and editor, Hector Charlesworth, put it: "Her genius is wholly Indian."

Pauline had little formal education, totalling no more than two years with a governess, three years at an Indian day school and two years at Central School in Brantford. In its place she had another kind of education—a gracious home life, the precept and example of cultured parents, and the company of brilliant, famous, and witty guests. Among these, as she relates in the last item in this book, was Prince Arthur of Connaught whom her father and grandfather made a Mohawk chieftain. Years later, as Duke of Connaught and Governor-General of Canada, he repaid this visit by interrupting a tour of Vancouver to sit for a while at the bedside of the dying writer and hold her hand in remembrance.

Her childhood home was a fine, big, stuccoed colonial mansion called Chiefswood, set in a well-wooded park overlooking the Grand River. Prepared by George Johnson for his bride, it was furnished in a manner to make her English heart happy, including a piano which was a rare luxury even in the homes of white Canadians in 1853. The library was well stocked and both her parents were discriminating readers, a habit they encouraged in Pauline who as a child was avidly reading Scott, Longfellow, Byron, Shakespeare, Addison, Dickens, and Emerson. There is a story of the nine-year-old Pauline surprising a visitor by asking for a book of verse when asked what treat she would like.

When she was twenty-three, Pauline was shaken out of her halcyon world of reading and dreaming by the death of her father, the result of a brutal beating at the hands of thugs who resented his efforts to halt their profitable traffic in raw whiskey among the Indians. The family could not afford Chiefswood, and the mother with her two daughters moved to Brantford. The two sons, Beverley and Allan, good-looking young men with fine scholastic records, were already working, one in Hamilton and the other in Toronto. The elder sister, Evelyn, got an office job in Brantford, and Pauline started sending out poems to various publications. Earlier she had written the occasional poem, and one of these, inscribed in the album of her school friend, Jean Morton, became her first published work, appearing as "My Little Jean" in the New York magazine *Gems of Poetry*, in 1885. Other poems appeared in other publications in Toronto, New York, and London and by 1889 she was well enough known to have two poems included in *Songs of the Great Dominion*, an anthology compiled by the Montreal lawyer-poet William D. Lighthall. This brought her work to the attention of the influential Theodore Watts-Dunton, who hailed this appearance of "a poet so rare—so full of the spirit of the open air."

Thus Pauline was started on her way, at an age when most poets are already getting their second wind. Her leisurely adolescence and late start are particularly to be regretted when we remember that she died a mere twenty-four years later—a period frittered away by financial worries and ill-health to little more than a decade of creative work.

Pauline was thirty-one when she was invited to Toronto to take part in a literary evening organized by Frank Yeigh, who later recalled: "The evening was dragging and the interest lessening when the Indian poet-princess glided to the platform, her dark eyes flashing and her sinewy form the essence of gracefulness. Then she gave the first rendition of 'Cry From An Indian Wife'—thrilling was the effect, dramatic the appeal of this dark-hued girl who seemed to personify her race. A tense stillness followed, then there broke unrestrained expressions of approval in tumultuous applause. Rarely does an audience so rapidly change its mood, and rarely does a reciter so capture her hearers. Tekahionwake leaped into fame that night."

During the next year Miss Johnson made 125 platform appearances in Ontario and Eastern Canada. From the proceeds, she was able to go to England in 1894 to arrange for the publication of her first book, *The White Wampum*, which was a critical success but brought her little money. Until the last year of her life Pauline made little more than $500 by her poetry alone. She found a more ready livelihood in a strenuous schedule of platform appearances that took her, during fifteen years, several times across Canada, deep into the United States and, on two further occasions, in 1906 and 1907, to England.

Those were the great days of platform entertainment, but Pauline contributed far more than entertainment. Wherever she went she brought her vision of a great and united Canada, rising above regional differences and petty racial loyalties. This in itself was a major contribution to Canada, and in a sense she sacrificed her literary career to it, putting her tours before literary production and abusing her great poetic gifts by turning out topical and jingoistic doggerel that served its purpose well but is worthless now. In spite of everything, and it must be remembered that travel in those days was not the swift and easy thing it is today, Pauline managed to turn out a handful of exquisite lyrics of great feeling and beauty. Her best poems express her loving, personal response to the natural beauty of water and trees, or are wistful and poignant love lyrics, full of unfulfilled longing and loneliness, illustrative of her own mysterious tragedy which saw her engaged but, for some unknown reason, never married.

However, it was not until she forsook the platform that her literary ability achieved its peak of expression. That was in 1909, when she settled in the Vancouver she had come to love. But it was far too late for the many ambitious projects she had in mind. The exhaustion she was feeling was not entirely due to her strenuous life but to a serious illness. Cancer had taken hold.

At this time her one consolation was the renewal of her friendship with Chief Joe Capilano who, during the last year of his life, became her *tillicum*, or great friend, as well as her guide into the customs and legends of his Squamish tribes. The first of these Legends to appear in print was "The Two Sisters" published in the Vancouver *Province* on April 16, 1910, shortly after Chief Joe had died. During the next year, twenty-two of Pauline's sketches appeared in the *Province*, of which sixteen were Indian legends, twelve of them drawn from Chief Joe's memory and the other four from Pauline's own store of Indian mythology. In 1911, the fifteen stories that appear in this book—including all twelve of Chief Joe's Vancouver legends—were published in Vancouver under the title *Legends of Vancouver*. Pauline had wanted them called "Legends of the Capilano" in tribute to her friend, but she was too ill to insist, which is just as well as the present title is more accurately descriptive. Instead, she inserted a 100-word foreword telling of her debt to Chief Joe, his role in the Legends, and mentioning that most of them were told in English for the first time.

During the last two years of her life Pauline was under almost constant sedation and, although she was not bed-ridden but was able to take walks and meet her friends, her mind was incapable of the concentrated effort necessary for creative work. She was comforted, however, by the knowledge that her Legends were selling —they sold ten thousand copies before her death—and that she was neither in want nor a burden on her friends.

Her last days were also brightened by the confident knowledge that her work would live. That it has survived the personal memories of those who had experienced her dramatic readings, the alternate fire and softness of her intonation, the lovely cadences of her voice, unspoiled by any elocution school, is a tribute to the intrinsic value of her work.

She was buried on March 10, 1913, her fifty-second birthday. The day was one of general mourning in Vancouver. Flags were at half-mast, civic offices were closed as the Mayor and aldermen joined the great throng of the high and the low who took part in the service at Christ Church. Wreathes and condolences poured in from the Governor-General, the Prime Minister and his Cabinet, the Royal Society of Canada, from groups and individuals in all parts of Canada, and from England. By special and unique dispensation, interment was in Stanley Park, where she had loved to walk, not far from the Siwash Rock she had made famous. Her memorials today are a simple cairn where several walks meet in Stanley Park, a rough stone in the graveyard of Brantford's Mohawk Chapel where her father and grandfather lie buried, and these *Legends of Vancouver* which enshrine some of the love and wisdom of the Indian race she lived to serve.

Marcus Van Steen

Brantford, Ontario
July, 1960

The Two Sisters

You can see them as you look towards the north and the west, where the dream hills swim into the sky amid their ever-drifting clouds of pearl and grey. They catch the earliest hint of sunrise, they hold the last colour of sunset. Twin mountains they are, lifting their twin peaks above the fairest city in all Canada, and known throughout the British Empire as "The Lions of Vancouver."

Sometimes the smoke of forest fires blurs them until they gleam like opals in a purple atmosphere, too beautiful for words to paint. Sometimes the slanting rains festoon scarfs of mist about their crests, and the peaks fade into shadowy outlines, melting, melting, forever melting into the distances. But for most days in the year the sun circles the twin glories with a sweep of gold. The moon washes them with a torrent of silver. Oftentimes, when the city is shrouded in rain, the sun yellows their snows to a deep orange; but through sun and shadow they stand immovable, smiling westward above the waters of the restless Pacific, eastward above the superb beauty of the Capilano Canyon. But the Indian tribes do not know these peaks as "The Lions." Even the Chief, whose feet have so recently wandered to the Happy Hunting Grounds, never heard the name given them until I mentioned it to him one dreamy August day, as together we followed the trail leading to the canyon. He seemed so surprised at the name that I mentioned the reason it had been applied to them, asking him if he recalled the Landseer Lions in Trafalgar Square. Yes, he remembered those splendid sculptures, and his quick eye saw the resemblance instantly. It appeared to please him, and his fine face expressed the haunting memories of the far-away roar of Old London. But the "call of the blood" was stronger, and presently he referred to the Indian legend of those peaks—a legend that I have reason to believe is absolutely unknown to thousands of

Palefaces who look upon "The Lions" daily, without the love for them that is in the Indian heart, without knowledge of the secret of "The Two Sisters." The legend was intensely fascinating as it left his lips in the quaint broken English that is never so dulcet as when it slips from an Indian tongue. His inimitable gestures, strong, graceful, comprehensive, were like a perfectly chosen frame embracing a delicate painting, and his brooding eyes were as the light in which the picture hung. "Many thousands of years ago," he began, "there were no twin peaks like sentinels guarding the outposts of this sunset coast. They were placed there long after the first creation, when the Sagalie Tyee moulded the mountains, and patterned the mighty rivers where the salmon run, because of His love for His Indian children, and His Wisdom for their necessities. In those times there were many and mighty Indian tribes along the Pacific—in the mountain ranges, at the shores and sources of the great Fraser River. Indian law ruled the land. Indian customs prevailed. Indian beliefs were regarded. Those were the legend-making ages when great things occurred to make the traditions we repeat to our children today. Perhaps the greatest of these traditions is the story of 'The Two Sisters, for they are known to us as 'The Chief's Daughters,' and to them we owe the Great Peace in which we live, and have lived for many countless moons. There is an ancient custom amongst the Coast tribes that when our daughters step from childhood into the great world of womanhood the occasion must be made one of extreme rejoicing. The being who possesses the possibility of someday mothering a man-child, a warrior, a brave, receives much consideration in most nations, but to us, the Sunset Tribes, she is honoured above all people. The parents usually give a great potlatch, and a feast that lasts many days. The entire tribe and the surrounding tribes are bidden to this festival. More than that, sometimes when a great Tyee celebrates for his daughter, the tribes from far up the coast, from the distant north, from inland, from the island, from the Cariboo country, are gathered as guests to the feast. During these days of rejoicing, the girl is placed in a high seat, an exalted position, for is she not marriageable? And does not marriage mean motherhood? And does not motherhood means a vaster nation of brave sons and of gentle daughters who, in their turn, will give us sons and daughters of their own?

"But it was many thousands of years ago that a great Tyee had two daughters that grew to womanhood at the same springtime, when the first great run of salmon thronged the rivers, and the ollallie bushes were heavy with blossoms. These two daughters were young, lovable, and oh! very beautiful. Their father, the great Tyee, prepared to make a feast such as the Coast had never seen. There were to be days and days of rejoicing, the people were to come for many leagues, were to bring gifts to the girls and to receive gifts of great value from the Chief, and hospitality was to reign as long as pleasuring feet could dance, and enjoying lips could laugh, and mouths partake of the excellence of the Chief's fish, game, and ollallies.

"The only shadow on the joy of it all was war, for the tribe of the great Tyee was at war with the Upper Coast Indians, those who lived north, near what is named by the Paleface as the port of Prince Rupert. Giant war canoes slipped along the entire coast, war parties paddled up and down, war songs broke the silences of the nights, hatred, vengeance, strife, horror festered everywhere like sores on the surface of the earth. But the great Tyee, after warring for weeks, turned and laughed at the battle and the bloodshed, for he had been victor in every encounter, and he could well afford to leave the strife for a brief week and feast in his daughters' honour, nor permit any mere enemy to come between him and the traditions of his race and household. So he turned insultingly deaf ears to

23

their war cries; he ignored with arrogant in-difference their paddle dips that encroached within his own coast waters, and he prepared, as a great Tyee should, to royally entertain his tribesmen in honour of his daughters.

"But seven suns before the great feast, these two maidens came before him, hand clasped in hand.

" 'Oh! our father,' they said, 'may we speak?'

" 'Speak, my daughters, my girls with the eyes of April, the hearts of June' " (early spring and early summer would be the more accurate Indian phrasing).

" 'Some day, Oh! our father, we may mother a man-child, who may grow to be just such a powerful Tyee as you are, and for this honour that may some day be ours we have come to crave a favour of you—you, Oh! our father.'

" 'It is your privilege at this celebration to receive any favour your hearts may wish,' he replied graciously, placing his fingers beneath their girlish chins. 'The favour is yours before you ask it, my daughters.'

" 'Will you, for our sakes, invite the great northern hostile tribe—the tribe you war upon —to this, our feast?' they asked fearlessly.

" 'To a peaceful feast, a feast in the honour of women?' he exclaimed incredulously.

" 'So we would desire it,' they answered.

" 'And so shall it be,' he declared. 'I can deny you nothing this day, and some time you may bear sons to bless this peace you have asked, and to bless their mother's sire for granting it.' Then he turned to all the young men of the tribe and commanded, 'Build fires at sunset on all the coast headlands—fires of welcome. Man your canoes and face the north, greet the enemy, and tell them that I, the Tyee of the Capilanos, ask —no, command that they join me for a great feast in honour of my two daughters.' And when the northern tribes got this invitation they flocked down the coast to this feast of a Great Peace. They brought their women and their children: they brought game and fish, gold and white stone beads, baskets and carven ladles, and wonderful woven blankets to lay at the feet of their now acknowledged ruler, the great Tyee. And he, in turn, gave such a pot-latch that nothing but tradition can vie with it. There were long, glad days of joyousness, long pleasurable nights of dancing and camp fires, and vast quantities of food. The war canoes were emptied of their deadly weapons and filled with the daily catch of salmon. The hostile war songs ceased, and in their place were heard the soft shuffle of dancing feet, the singing voices of women, the play-games of the children of two

25

powerful tribes which had been until now ancient enemies, for a great and lasting brotherhood was sealed between them—their war songs were ended forever.

"Then the Sagalie Tyee smiled on His Indian children: 'I will make these young-eyed maidens immortal,' He said. In the cup of His hands he lifted the Chief's two daughters and set them forever in a high place, for they had borne two offspring—Peace and Brotherhood—each of which is now a great Tyee ruling this land.

"And on the mountain crest the Chief's daughters can be seen wrapped in the suns, the snows, the stars of all seasons, for they have stood in this high place for thousands of years, and will stand for thousands of years to come, guarding the peace of the Pacific Coast and the quiet of the Capilano Canyon."

*　　　*　　　*　　　*

This is the Indian legend of "The Lions of Vancouver" as I had it from one who will tell me no more the traditions of his people.

The Siwash Rock

Unique, and so distinct from its surroundings as to suggest rather the handicraft of man than a whim of Nature, it looms up at the entrance to the Narrows, a symmetrical column of solid grey stone. There are no similar formations within the range of vision, or indeed within many a day's paddle up and down the coast. Amongst all the wonders, the natural beauties that encircle Vancouver, the marvels of mountains shaped into crouching lions and brooding beavers, the yawning canyons, the stupendous forest firs and cedars, Siwash Rock stands as distinct, as individual, as if dropped from another sphere.

I saw it first in the slanting light of a redly

29

setting August sun; the little tuft of green shrubbery that crests its summit was black against the crimson of sea and sky, and its colossal base of grey stone gleamed like flaming polished granite.

My old tillicum lifted his paddle blade to point towards it. "You know the story?" he asked. I shook my head (experience had taught me his love of silent replies, his moods of legend-telling). For a time we paddled slowly; the rock detached itself from its background of forest and shore, and it stood forth like a sentinel—erect, enduring, eternal.

"Do you think it stands straight—like a man?" he asked.

"Yes, like some noble-spirited, upright warrior," I replied.

"It is a man," he said, "and a warrior man, too; a man who fought for everything that was noble and upright."

"What do you regard as everything that is noble and upright, Chief?" I asked, curious as to his ideas. I shall not forget the reply: it was but two words—astounding, amazing words. He said simply:

"Clean fatherhood."

Through my mind raced tumultuous recollections of numberless articles in yet numberless magazines, all dealing with the recent "fad" of motherhood, but I had to hear from the lips of a Squamish Indian chief the only treatise on the nobility of "clean fatherhood" that I have yet unearthed. And this treatise has been an Indian legend for centuries; and lest they forget how all-important those two little words must ever be, Siwash Rock stands to remind them, set there by the Deity as a monument to one who kept his own life clean, that cleanliness might be the heritage of the generations to come.

It was "thousands of years ago" (all Indian legends begin in extremely remote times) that a handsome boy chief journeyed in his canoe to the upper coast for the shy little northern girl whom he brought home as his wife. Boy though he was, the young chief had proved himself to be an excellent warrior, a fearless hunter, and an upright, courageous man among men. His tribe loved him, his enemies respected him, and the base and mean and cowardly feared him.

The customs and traditions of his ancestors were a positive religion to him, the sayings and the advices of the old people were his creed. He was conservative in every rite and ritual of his race. He fought his tribal enemies like the savage that he was. He sang his war songs, danced his war dances, slew his foes, but the little girl-wife from the north he treated with the deference that he gave his own mother, for was she not to be the mother of his warrior son?

The year rolled round, weeks merged into months, winter into spring, and one glorious summer at daybreak he wakened to her voice calling him. She stood beside him, smiling.

"It will be today," she said proudly.

He sprang from his couch of wolf skins and looked out upon the coming day: the promise of what it would bring him seemed breathing through all his forest world. He took her very gently by the hand and led her through the tangle of wilderness down to the water's edge, where the beauty spot we moderns call Stanley Park bends about Prospect Point. "I must swim," he told her.

"I must swim, too," she smiled with the perfect understanding of two beings who are mated. For to them the old Indian custom was law—the custom that the parents of a coming child must swim until their flesh is so clear and clean that a wild animal cannot scent their proximity. If the wild creatures of the forests have no fear of them, then, and only then, are they fit to become parents, and to scent a human is in itself a fearsome thing to all wild creatures.

So those two plunged into the waters of the Narrows as the grey dawn slipped up the eastern skies and all the forest awoke to the life of a new, glad day. Presently he took her ashore, and smilingly she crept away under the giant trees. "I must be alone," she said, "but come to me at sunrise : you will not find me alone then." He smiled also, and plunged back into the sea. He must swim, swim, swim through this hour when his fatherhood was coming upon him. It was the law that he must be clean, spotlessly clean, so that when his child looked out upon the world it would have the chance to live its own life clean. If he did not swim hour upon hour his child would come to an unclean father. He must give his child a chance in life; he must not hamper it by his own uncleanliness at its birth. It was the tribal law—the law of vicarious purity.

As he swam joyously to and fro, a canoe bearing Four Men headed up the Narrows. These men were giants in stature, and the stroke of their paddles made huge eddies that boiled like the seething tides.

"Out from our course!" they cried as his lithe, copper-coloured body arose and fell with his splendid stroke. He laughed at them, giants though they were, and answered that he could not cease his swimming at their demand.

"But you shall cease!" they commanded. "We are the men (agents) of the Sagalie Tyee (God), and we command you ashore out of our

33

way!" (I find in all these Coast Indian legends that the Deity is represented by Four Men usually paddling an immense canoe.)

He ceased swimming and, lifting his head, defied them. "I shall not stop, nor yet go ashore," he declared, striking out once more to the middle of the channel.

"Do you dare disobey us," they cried—"we, the men of the Sagalie Tyee? We can turn you into a fish, or a tree, or a stone for this; do you dare disobey the Great Tyee?"

"I dare anything for the cleanliness and purity of my coming child. I dare even the Sagalie Tyee Himself, but my child must be born to a spotless life."

The Four Men were astounded. They consulted together, lighted their pipes and sat in council. Never had they, the men of the Sagalie Tyee, been defied before. Now, for the sake of a little, unborn child, they were ignored, disobeyed, almost despised. The lithe young copper-coloured body still disported itself in the cool waters; superstition held that should their canoe, or even their paddle blades, touch a human being their marvellous power would be lost. The handsome young chief swam directly in their course. They dared not run him down; if so, they would become as other men. While they yet counselled what to do, there floated from out the forest a faint, strange, compelling sound. They listened, and the young chief ceased his stroke as he listened also. The faint sound drifted out across the waters once more. It was the cry of a little, little child. Then one of the Four Men, he that steered the canoe, the strongest and tallest of them all, arose and, standing erect, stretched out his arms towards the rising sun and chanted, not a curse on the young chief's disobedience, but a promise of everlasting days and freedom from death.

"Because you have defied all things that came in your path we promise this to you," he chanted; "you have defied what interferes with your child's chance for a clean life, you have lived as you wish your son to live, you have defied us when we would have stopped your swimming and hampered your child's future. You have placed that child's future before all things, and for this the Sagalie Tyee commands us to make you forever a pattern for your tribe. You shall never die, but you shall stand through all the thousands of years to come, where all eyes can see you. You shall live, live, live as an indestructible monument to Clean Fatherhood."

The Four Men lifted their paddles and the handsome young chief swam inshore; as his feet touched the line where sea and land met, he was transformed into stone.

Then the Four Men said, "His wife and child must ever be near him; they shall not die, but live also." And they, too, were turned into stone. If you penetrate the hollows in the woods near Siwash Rock you will find a large rock and a smaller one beside it. They are the shy little bride-wife from the north, with her hour-old baby beside her. And from the uttermost parts of the world vessels come daily throbbing and sailing up the Narrows. From far trans-Pacific ports, from the frozen North, from the lands of the Southern Cross, they pass and re-pass the living rock that was there before their hulls were shaped, that will be there when their very names are forgotten, when their crews and their captains have taken their long last voyage, when their merchandise has rotted, and their owners are known no more. But the tall, grey column of stone will still be there—a monument to one man's fidelity to a generation yet unborn—and will endure from everlasting to everlasting.

The Recluse

Journeying towards the upper course of the Capilano River, about a mile citywards from the dam, you will pass a disused logger's shack. Leave the trail at this point and strike through the undergrowth for a few hundred yards to the left, and you will be on the rocky borders of that purest, most restless river in all Canada. The stream is haunted with tradition, teeming with a score of romances that vie with its grandeur and loveliness, and of which its waters are perpetually whispering. But I learned this legend from one whose voice was as dulcet as the swirling rapids; but, unlike them, that voice is hushed today, while the river still sings on— sings on.

It was singing in very melodious tones through the long August afternoon two summers ago, while we, the chief, his happy-hearted wife and bright, young daughter, all lounged amongst the boulders and watched the lazy clouds drift from peak to peak far above us. It was one of his inspired days; legends crowded to his lips as a whistle teases the mouth of a happy boy, his heart was brimming with tales of the bygones, his eyes were dark with dreams and that strange mournfulness that always haunted them when he spoke of long-ago romances. There was not a tree, a boulder, a dash of rapid upon which his glance fell which he could not link with some ancient poetic superstition. Then abruptly, in the very midst of his verbal reveries, he turned and asked me if I were superstitious. Of course I replied that I was.

"Do you think some happenings will bring trouble later on—will foretell evil?" he asked.

I made some evasive answer, which, however, seemed to satisfy him, for he plunged into the strange tale of the recluse of the canyon

40

with more vigour than dreaminess; but first he asked me the question :

"What do your own tribes, those east of the great mountains, think of twin children?"

I shook my head.

"That is enough," he said before I could reply. "I see, your people do not like them."

"Twin children are almost unknown with us," I hastened. "They are rare, very rare; but it is true we do not welcome them."

"Why?" he asked abruptly.

I was a little uncertain about telling him. If I said the wrong thing, the coming tale might die on his lips before it was born to speech, but we understood each other so well that I finally ventured the truth :

"We Iroquois say that twin children are as rabbits," I explained. "The nation always nicknames the parents 'Tow-wan-da-na-ga ' That is the Mohawk for rabbit."

"Is that all?" he asked curiously.

"That is all. Is it not enough to render twin children unwelcome?" I questioned.

He thought awhile, then with evident desire to learn how all races regarded this occurrence, he said, "You have been much among the Palefaces, what do they say of twins?"

"Oh! the Palefaces like them. They are— they are—oh! well, they say they are very proud of having twins," I stammered. Once again I was hardly sure of my ground. He looked most incredulous, and I was led to enquire what his own people of the Squamish thought of this discussed problem.

"It is no pride to us," he said decidedly; "nor yet is it disgrace of rabbits, but it is a fearsome thing—a sign of coming evil to the father and, worse than that, of coming disaster to the tribe."

Then I knew he held in his heart some strange incident that gave substance to the superstition. "Won't you tell it to me?" I begged.

He leaned a little backwards against a giant boulder, clasping his thin, brown hands about his knees; his eyes roved up the galloping river, then swept down the singing waters to where they crowded past the sudden bend, and during the entire recital of the strange legend his eyes never left that spot where the stream disappeared in its hurrying journey to the sea. Without preamble he began:

"It was a grey morning when they told him of this disaster that had befallen him. He was a great chief, and he ruled many tribes on the North Pacific Coast; but what was his greatness now? His young wife had borne him twins, and was sobbing out her anguish in the little fir-bark lodge near the tidewater.

"Beyond the doorway gathered many old men and women—old in years, old in wisdom, old in the lore and learning of their nations. Some of them wept, some chanted solemnly the dirge of their lost hopes and happiness, which would never return because of this calamity; others discussed in hushed voices this awesome thing, and for hours their grave council was broken only by the infant cries of the two boy-babies in the bark lodge, the hopeless sobs of the young mother, the agonized moans of the stricken chief—their father.

" 'Something dire will happen to the tribe.' said the old men in council.

" 'Something dire will happen to him, my husband,' wept the afflicted young mother.

" 'Something dire will happen to us all,' echoed the unhappy father.

"Then an ancient medicine man arose, lifting his arms, outstretching his palms to hush the lamenting throng. His voice shook with the weight of many winters, but his eyes were yet keen and mirrored the clear thought and brain behind them, as the still trout pools in the Capilano mirror the mountain tops. His words were masterful, his gestures commanding, his shoulders erect and kindly. His was a personality and an inspiration that no one dared dispute, and his judgement was accepted as the words fell slowly, like a doom.

" 'It is the olden law of the Squamish that lest evil befall the tribe the sire of twin children must go afar and alone into the mountain fastnesses, there by his isolation and his loneliness to prove himself stronger than the threatened evil, and thus to beat back the shadow that would otherwise follow him and all his people. I, therefore, name for him the length of days that he must spend alone fighting his invisible enemy. He will know by some great sign in Nature the hour that the evil is conquered, the hour that his race is saved. He must leave before this sun sets, taking with him only his strongest bow, his fleetest arrows, and going up into the mountain wilderness remain there ten days— alone, alone.'

"The masterful voice ceased, the tribe wailed their assent, the father arose speechless, his drawn face revealing great agony over this seemingly brief banishment. He took leave of his sobbing wife, of the two tiny souls that were his sons, grasped his favourite bow and arrows, and faced the forest like a warrior. But at the end of the ten days he did not return, nor yet ten weeks, nor yet ten months.

" 'He is dead,' wept the mother into the baby ears of her two boys. 'He could not battle

44

against the evil that threatened; it was stronger than he—he so strong, so proud, so brave.'

" 'He is dead,' echoed the tribesmen and the tribeswoman. 'Our strong, brave chief, he is dead.' So they mourned the long year through, but their chants and their tears but renewed their grief; he did not return to them.

"Meanwhile, far up the Capilano the banished chief had built his solitary home; for who can tell what fatal trick of sound, what current of air, what faltering note in the voice of the medicine man had deceived his alert Indian ears? But some unhappy fate had led him to understand that his solitude must be of ten years' duration, not ten days, and he had accepted the mandate with the heroism of a stoic. For if he had refused to do so his belief was that, although the threatened disaster would be spared him, the evil would fall upon his tribe. Thus was one more added to the long list of self-forgetting souls whose creed has been, 'It is fitting that one should suffer for the people.' It was the world-old heroism of vicarious sacrifice.

"With his hunting-knife the banished Squamish chief stripped the bark from the firs and cedars, building for himself a lodge beside the Capilano River, where leaping trout and salmon could be speared by arrow-heads fastened to deftly shaped, long handles. All through the salmon run he smoked and dried the fish with the care of a housewife. The mountain sheep and goats, and even huge black and cinnamon bears, fell before his unerring arrows; the fleet-footed deer never returned to their haunts from their evening drinking at the edge of the stream —their wild hearts, their agile bodies were stilled when he took aim. Smoked hams and saddles hung in rows from the cross poles of his bark lodge, and the magnificent pelts of animals carpeted his floors, padded his couch and clothed his body. He tanned the soft doe hides, making leggings, moccasins and shirts, stitching them together with deer sinew as he had seen his mother do in the long-ago. He gathered the juicy salmonberries, their acid a sylvan, healthful change from meat and fish. Month by month and year by year he sat beside his lonely camp fire, waiting for his long term of solitude to end. One comfort alone was his —he was enduring the disaster, fighting the evil, that his tribe might go unscathed, that his people be saved from calamity. Slowly, laboriously the tenth year dawned; day by day it dragged its long weeks across his waiting heart, for Nature had not yet given the sign that his long probation was over.

"Then one hot summer day the Thunder

Bird came crashing through the mountains about him. Up from the arms of the Pacific rolled the storm cloud, and the Thunder Bird, with its eyes of flashing light, beat its huge vibrating wings on crag and canyon.

"Upstream, a tall shaft of granite rears it needle-like length. It is named 'Thunder Rock,' and wise men of the Paleface people say it is rich in ore—copper, silver, and gold. At the base of this shaft the Squamish chief crouched when the storm cloud broke and bellowed through the ranges, and on its summit the Thunder Bird perched, its gigantic wings threshing the air into booming sounds, into splitting terrors, like the crash of a giant cedar hurtling down the mountain side.

"But when the beating of those black pinions ceased and the echo of their thunder waves died down the depths of the canyon, the Squamish chief arose as a new man. The shadow on his soul had lifted, the fears of evil were cowed and conquered. In his brain, his blood, his veins, his sinews, he felt that the poison of melancholy dwelt no more. He had redeemed his fault of fathering twin children; he had fulfilled the demands of the law of his tribe.

"As he heard the last beat of the Thunder Bird's wings dying slowly, slowly, faintly, faintly, among the crags, he knew that the bird, too, was dying, for its soul was leaving its monster black body, and presently that soul appeared in the sky. He could see it arching overhead, before it took its long journey to the Happy Hunting Grounds, for the soul of the Thunder Bird was a radiant half-circle of glorious colour spanning from peak to peak. He lifted his head then, for he knew it was the sign the ancient medicine man had told him to wait for—the sign that his long banishment was ended.

"And all these years, down in the tidewater country, the little brown-faced twins were asking childwise, 'Where is our father? Why have we no father, like other boys?' To be met only with the oft-repeated reply, 'Your father is no more. Your father, the great chief, is dead.'

"But some strange filial intuition told the boys that their sire would some day return. Often they voiced this feeling to their mother, but she would only weep and say that not even the witchcraft of the great medicine man could bring him to them. But when they were ten years old the two children came to their mother, hand within hand. They were armed with their little hunting-knives, their salmon spears, their tiny bows and arrows.

" 'We go to find our father,' they said.

" 'Oh! useless quest,' wailed the mother.

" 'Oh! useless quest,' echoed the tribespeople.

"But the great medicine man said, 'The heart of a child has invisible eyes, perhaps the child-eyes see him. The heart of a child has invisible ears, perhaps the child-ears hear him call. Let them go.' So the little children went forth into the forest; their young feet flew as though shod with wings, their young hearts pointed to the north as does the white man's compass. Day after day they journeyed upstream, until rounding a sudden bend they beheld a bark lodge with a thin blue curl of smoke drifting from its roof.

" 'It is our father's lodge,' they told each other, for their childish hearts were unerring in response to the call of kinship. Hand-in-hand they approached, and entering the lodge, said the one word, 'Come.'

"The great Squamish chief outstretched his arms towards them, then towards the laughing river, then towards the mountains.

" 'Welcome, my sons!' he said. 'And good-bye, my mountains, my brothers, my crags and my canyons!' And with a child clinging to each hand he faced once more the country of the tidewater."

*　　*　　*　　*

The legend was ended.

For a long time he sat in silence. He had removed his gaze from the bend in the river, around which the two children had come and where the eyes of the recluse had first rested on them after ten years of solitude.

The chief spoke again, "It was here, on this spot we are sitting, that he built his lodge: here he dwelt those ten years alone, alone."

I nodded silently. The legend was too beautiful to mar with comments, and as the twilight fell, we threaded our way through the underbrush, past the disused logger's camp and into the trail that leads citywards.

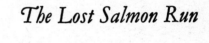

The Lost Salmon Run

Great had been the "run," and the sockeye season was almost over. For that reason I wondered many times why my old friend, the klootchman, had failed to make one of the fishing fleet. She was an indefatigable work-woman, rivalling her husband as an expert catcher, and all the year through she talked of little else but the coming run. But this especial season she had not appeared amongst her fellow-kind. The fleet and the canneries knew nothing of her, and when I enquired of her tribespeople they would reply without explanation, "She not here this year."

But one russet September afternoon I found her. I had idled down the trail from the swans' basin in Stanley Park to the rim that skirts the Narrows, and I saw her graceful, high-bowed canoe heading for the beach that is the favourite landing-place of the "tillicums" from the Mission. Her canoe looked like a dream-craft, for the water was very still, and everywhere a blue film hung like a fragrant veil, for the peat on Lulu Island had been smouldering for days and its pungent odours and blue-grey haze made a dream-world of sea and shore and sky.

I hurried upshore, hailing her in the Chinook, and as she caught my voice she lifted her paddle directly above her head in the Indian signal of greeting.

As she beached, I greeted her with extended eager hands to assist her ashore, for the klootchman is getting to be an old woman; albeit she paddles against tidewater like a boy in his teens.

"No," she said, as I begged her to come ashore. "I not wait—me. I just come to fetch Maarda; she been city; she come soon—now." But she left her "working" attitude and curled like a schoolgirl in the bow of the canoe, her elbows resting on her paddle which she had flung across the gunwales.

"I have missed you, klootchman; you have not been to see me for three moons, and you

54

have not fished or been at the canneries," I remarked.

"No," she said. "I stay home this year." Then leaning towards me with grave import in her manner, her eyes, her voice, she added, "I have a grandchild, born first week July, so—I stay."

So this explained her absence. I, of course, offered congratulations and enquired all about the great event, for this was her first grandchild, and the little person was of importance.

"And are you going to make a fisherman of him?" I asked.

"No, no, not boy-child, it is girl-child," she answered with some indescribable trick of expression that led me to know she preferred it so.

"You are pleased it is a girl?" I questioned in surprise.

"Very pleased," she replied emphatically. "Very good luck to have girl for first grandchild. Our tribe not like yours: we want girl children first; we not always wish boy-child born just for fight. Your people, they care only for war-path; our tribe more peaceful. Very good sign first grandchild to be girl. I tell you why: girl-child maybe some time mother herself; very grand thing to be mother."

I felt I had caught the secret of her meaning. She was rejoicing that this little one should some time become one of the mothers of her race. We chatted over it a little longer and she gave me several playful "digs" about my own tribe thinking so much less of motherhood than hers, and so much more of battle and bloodshed. Then we drifted into talk of the sockeye run and of the hyiu chickimin the Indians would get.

"Yes, hyiu chickimin," she repeated with a sigh of satisfaction. "Always; and hyiu muck-a-muck when big salmon run. No more ever come that bad year when not any fish."

"When was that?" I asked.

"Before you born, or I, or"—pointing across the park to the distant city of Vancouver, that breathed its wealth and beauty across the September afternoon—"before that place born, before white man come here—oh! long before."

Dear old klootchman! I knew by the dusk in her eyes that she was back in her Land of Legends, and that soon I would be the richer in my hoard of Indian lore. She sat, still leaning on her paddle; her eyes, half-closed, rested on the distant outline of the blurred heights across the Inlet. I shall not further attempt her broken English, for this is but the shadow of her story, and without her unique personality the legend is as a flower that lacks both colour and fragrance. She called it "The Lost Salmon Run."

"The wife of the Great Tyee was but a wisp of a girl, but all the world was young in those days; even the Fraser River was young and small, not the mighty water it is today; but the pink salmon crowded its throat just as they do now, and the tillicums caught and salted and smoked the fish just as they have done this year, just as they will always do. But it was yet winter, and the rains were slanting and the fogs drifting, when the wife of the Great Tyee stood before him and said:

" 'Before the salmon run I shall give to you a great gift. Will you honour me most if it is the gift of a boy-child or a girl-child?' The Great Tyee loved the woman. He was stern with his people, hard with his tribe; he ruled his council fires with a will of stone. His medicine men said he had no human heart in his body; his warriors said he had no human blood in his veins. But he clasped this woman's hands, and his eyes, his lips, his voice, were gentle as her own, as he replied:

" 'Give to me a girl-child—a little girl-child —that she may grow to be like you and, in her turn, give to her husband children.'

"But when the tribespeople heard of his choice they arose in great anger. They surrounded him in a deep, indignant circle. 'You are a slave to the woman,' they declared, 'and now you desire to make yourself a slave to a woman-baby. We want an heir—a man-child to be our Great Tyee in years to come. When you are old and weary of tribal affairs, when you sit wrapped in your blanket in the hot summer sunshine, because your blood is old and thin, what can a girl-child do to help either you or us? Who, then, will be our Great Tyee?'

"He stood in the centre of the menacing circle, his arms folded, his chin raised, his eyes hard as flint. His voice, cold as stone, replied:

" 'Perhaps she will give you such a man-child and, if so, the child is yours; he will belong to you, not to me; he will become the possession of the people. But if the child is a girl she will belong to me—she will be mine. You cannot take her from me as you took me from my mother's side and forced me to forget my aged father in my service to my tribe; she will belong to me, will be the mother of my grandchildren, and her husband will be my son.'

" 'You do not care for the good of your tribe. You care only for your own wishes and desires,' they rebelled. 'Suppose the salmon run is small, we will have no food; suppose there is no man-child, we will have no Great Tyee to show us how to get food from other tribes, and we shall starve.'

" 'Your hearts are black and bloodless,' thundered the Great Tyee, turning upon them fiercely, 'and your eyes are blinded. Do you wish the tribe to forget how great is the importance of a child that will some day be a mother herself, and give to your children and grandchildren a Great Tyee? Are the people to live, to thrive, to increase, to become more powerful with no mother-women to bear future sons and daughters? Your minds are dead, your brains are chilled. Still, even in your ignorance, you are my people: you and your wishes must be considered. I call together the great medicine men, the men of witchcraft, the men of magic. They shall decide the laws which will follow the bearing of either boy or girl-child. What say you, oh! mighty men?'

"Messengers were then sent up and down the coast, sent far up the Fraser River, and to the valley lands inland for many leagues, gathering as they journeyed all the men of magic that could be found. Never were so many medicine men in council before. They built fires and danced and chanted for many days. They spoke with the gods of the mountains, with the gods of the sea, then 'the power' of decision came to them. They were inspired with a choice to lay

59

before the tribespeople, and the most ancient medicine man in all the coast region arose and spoke their resolution:

" 'The people of the tribe cannot be allowed to have all things. They want a boy-child and they want a great salmon run also. They cannot have both. The Sagalie Tyee has revealed to us, the great men of magic, that both these things will make the people arrogant and selfish. They must choose between the two.'

" 'Choose, oh! you ignorant tribespeople,' commanded the Great Tyee. 'The wise men of our Coast have said that the girl-child who will some day bear children of her own, will also bring abundance of salmon at her birth; but the boy-child brings to you but himself.'

" 'Let the salmon go,' shouted the people, 'but give us a future Great Tyee. Give us the boy-child.'

"And when the child was born it was a boy.

" 'Evil will fall upon you,' wailed the Great Tyee. 'You have despised a mother-woman. You will suffer evil and starvation and hunger and poverty, oh! foolish tribespeople. Did you not know how great a girl-child is?'

"That spring, people from a score of tribes came up to the Fraser for the salmon run. They came great distances—from the mountains, the lakes, the far-off dry lands, but not one fish entered the vast rivers of the Pacific Coast. The people had made their choice. They had forgotten the honour that a mother-child would have brought them. They were bereft of their food. They were stricken with poverty. Through the long winter that followed they endured hunger and starvation. Since then our tribe has always welcomed girl-children—we want no more lost runs."

The klootchman lifted her arms from her paddle as she concluded; her eyes left the irregular outline of the violet mountains. She had come back to this year of grace—her Legend Land had vanished.

"So," she added, "you see now, maybe, why I glad my grandchild is girl: it means big salmon run next year."

"It is a beautiful story, klootchman," I said, "and I feel a cruel delight that your men of magic punished the people for their ill-choice."

"That because you girl-child yourself," she laughed.

There was the slightest whisper of a step behind me. I turned to find Maarda almost at my elbow. The rising tide was unbeaching the canoe, and as Maarda stepped in and the klootchman slipped astern, it drifted afloat.

"Kla-how-ya," nodded the klootchman as she dipped her paddle-blade in exquisite silence.

"Kla-how-ya," smiled Maarda.

"Kla-how-ya, tillicums," I replied, and watched for many moments as they slipped away into the blurred distance, until the canoe merged into the violet and grey of the farther shore.

The Deep Waters

Far over your left shoulder as your boat leaves the Narrows to thread the beautiful waterways that lead to Vancouver Island, you will see the summit of Mount Baker robed in its everlasting whiteness and always reflecting some wonderful glory from the rising sun, the golden noontide, or the violet and amber sunset. This is the Mount Ararat of the Pacific Coast peoples; for those readers who are familiar with the ways and beliefs and faiths of primitive races will agree that it is difficult to discover anywhere in the world a race that has not some story of the Deluge, which they have chronicled and localized to fit the understanding and the conditions of the nation that composes their own immediate world.

Amongst the red nations of America I doubt if any two tribes have the same ideas regarding

65

the Flood. Some of the traditions concerning this vast whim of Nature are grotesque in the extreme; some are impressive; some even profound; but of all the stories of the Deluge that I have been able to collect I know of not a single one that can even begin to equal in beauty of conception, let alone rival in possible reality and truth, the Squamish legend of "The Deep Waters."

I here quote the legend of "mine own people," the Iroquois tribes of Ontario, regarding the Deluge. I do this to paint the colour of contrast in richer shades, for I am bound to admit that we who pride ourselves on ancient intellectuality have but a childish tale of the Flood when compared with the jealously preserved annals of the Squamish, which savour more of history than tradition. With "mine own people," animals always play a much more important part and are endowed with a finer intelligence than humans. I do not find amid my notes a single tradition of the Iroquois wherein animals do not figure, and our story of the Deluge rests entirely with the intelligence of sea-going and river-going creatures. With us, animals in olden times were greater than man; but it is not so with the Coast Indians, except in rare instances.

When a Coast Indian consents to tell you a

legend he will, without variation, begin it with, "It was before the white people came."

The natural thing for you then to ask is, "But who were here then?"

He will reply, "Indians, and just the trees, and animals, and fishes, and a few birds."

So you are prepared to accept the animal world as intelligent co-habitants of the Pacific slope, but he will not lead you to think he regards them as equals, much less superiors. But to revert to "mine own people": they hold the intelligence of wild animals far above that of man, for perhaps the one reason that when an animal is sick it effects its own cure; it knows what grasses and herbs to eat, what to avoid, while the sick human calls the medicine man, whose wisdom is not only the result of years of study, but also heredity; consequently any great natural event, such as the Deluge, has much to do with the wisdom of the creatures of the forests and the rivers.

Iroquois tradition tells us that once this earth was entirely submerged in water, and during this period for many days a busy little muskrat swam about vainly looking for a foothold of earth wherein to build his house. In his search he encountered a turtle also leisurely swimming, so they had speech together, and the muskrat complained of weariness; he could find no foothold;

he was tired of incessant swimming, and longed for land such as his ancestors enjoyed. The turtle suggested that the muskrat should dive and endeavour to find earth at the bottom of the sea. Acting on this advice the muskrat plunged down, then arose with his two little forepaws grasping some earth he had found beneath the waters.

"Place it on my shell and dive again for more," directed the turtle. The muskrat did so, but when he returned with his paws filled with earth he discovered the small quantity he had first deposited on the turtle's shell had doubled in size. The return from the third trip found the turtle's load again doubled. So the building went on at double compound increase, and the world grew its continents and its islands with great rapidity, and now rests on the shell of a turtle.

If you ask an Iroquois, "And did no men survive this flood?" he will reply, "Why should men survive? The animals are wiser than men; let the wisest live."

How, then, was the earth repeopled?

The Iroquois will tell you that the otter was a medicine man; that in swimming and diving about he found corpses of men and women; he sang his medicine songs and they came to life, and the otter brought them fish for food until they were strong enough to provide for themselves. Then the Iroquois will conclude his tale with, "You know well that the otter has greater wisdom than a man."

So much for "mine own people" and our profound respect for the superior intelligence of our little brothers of the animal world.

But the Squamish tribe hold other ideas. It was on a February day that I first listened to this beautiful, humane story of the Deluge. My royal old tillicum had come to see me through the rains and mists of late winter days. The gateways of my wigwam always stood open—very widely open—for his feet to enter, and this especial day he came with the worst downpour of the season.

Womanlike, I protested with a thousand contradictions in my voice that he should venture out to see me on such a day. It was "Oh! Chief, I am so glad to see you" and it was "Oh! Chief, why didn't you stay at home on such a wet day —your poor throat will suffer." But I soon had quantities of hot tea for him, and the huge cup my own father always used was his—as long as the Sagalie Tyee allowed his dear feet to wander my way. The immense cup stands idle and empty now for the second time.

Helping him off with his great-coat, I chatted on about the deluge of rain, and he remarked it was not so very bad, as one could yet walk.

"Fortunately, yes, for I cannot swim," I told him.

He laughed, replying, "Well, it is not so bad as when the Great Deep Waters covered the world."

Immediately I foresaw the coming legend, so crept into the shell of monosyllables.

"No?" I questioned.

"No," he replied. "For one time there was no land here at all; everywhere there was just water."

"I can quite believe it," I remarked caustically.

He laughed—that irresistible, though silent, David Warfield laugh of his that always brought a responsive smile from his listeners. Then he plunged directly into the tradition, with no preface save a comprehensive sweep of his wonderful hands towards my wide window, against which the rains were beating.

"It was after a long, long time of this—this rain. The mountain streams were swollen, the rivers choked, the sea began to rise—and yet it rained; for weeks and weeks it rained." He ceased speaking, while the shadows of centuries gone crept into his eyes. Tales of the misty past always inspired him.

"Yes," he continued. "It rained for weeks and weeks, while the mountain torrents roared thunderingly down, and the sea crept silently up. The level lands were first to float in sea water, then to disappear. The slopes were next to slip into the sea. The world was slowly being flooded. Hurriedly the Indian tribes gathered in one spot, a place of safety far above the reach of the on-creeping sea. The spot was the circling shore of Lake Beautiful, up the North Arm. They held a Great Council and decided at once upon a plan of action. A giant canoe should be built, and some means contrived to anchor it in case the waters mounted to the heights. The men undertook the canoe, the women the anchorage.

"A giant tree was felled, and day and night the men toiled over its construction into the most stupendous canoe the world has ever known. Not an hour, not a moment, but many worked, while the toil-wearied ones slept, only to awake to renewed toil. Meanwhile the women also worked at a cable—the largest, the longest, the strongest that Indian hands and teeth had ever made. Scores of them gathered and prepared the cedar fibre; scores of them plaited, rolled and seasoned it; scores of them chewed upon it inch by inch to make it pliable; scores of them oiled and worked, oiled and worked, oiled and worked it into a sea-resisting fabric. And still the sea crept up, and up, and up. It was the last day; hope of life for the tribe, of land for the world, was doomed. Strong hands, self-sacrificing hands fastened the cable the women had made—one end to the giant canoe, the other about an enormous boulder, a vast immovable rock as firm as the foundations of the world—for might not the canoe with its priceless freight drift out, far out, to sea, and when the water subsided might not this ship of safety be leagues and leagues beyond the sight of land on the storm-driven Pacific?

"Then with the bravest hearts that ever beat, noble hands lifted every child of the tribe into this vast canoe; not one single baby was overlooked. The canoe was stocked with food and fresh water, and lastly, the ancient men and women of the race selected as guardians to these children the bravest, most stalwart, handsomest young man of the tribe, and the mother of the youngest baby in the camp—she was but a girl of sixteen, her child but two weeks old; but she, too, was brave and very beautiful. These two were placed, she at the bow of the canoe to watch, he at the stern to guide, and all the little children crowded between.

"And still the sea crept up, and up, and up. At the crest of the bluffs about Lake Beautiful the doomed tribes crowded. Not a single person attempted to enter the canoe. There was no wailing, no crying out for safety. 'Let the little children, the young mother, and the bravest and best of our young men live,' was all the farewell those in the canoe heard as the waters reached the summit, and—the canoe floated. Last of all to be seen was the top of the tallest tree, then —all was a world of water.

"For days and days there was no land—just the rush of swirling, snarling sea; but the canoe rode safely at anchor, the cable those scores of dead, faithful women had made held true as the hearts that beat behind the toil and labour of it all.

"But one morning at sunrise, far to the south a speck floated on the breast of the waters; at midday it was larger; at evening it was yet larger. The moon arose, and in its magic light the man at the stern saw it was a patch of land. All night he watched it grow, and at daybreak looked with glad eyes upon the summit of Mount Baker. He cut the cable, grasped his paddle in his strong, young hands and steered for the south. When they landed, the waters were sunken half down the mountain side. The children were lifted out; the beautiful young mother, the stalwart young brave, turned to each other, clasped hands, looked into each others eyes—and smiled.

"And down in the vast country that lies between Mount Baker and the Fraser River they made a new camp, built new lodges, where the little children grew and thrived, and lived and loved, and the earth was repeopled by them.

"The Squamish say that in a gigantic crevice halfway to the crest of Mount Baker may yet be seen the outlines of an enormous canoe, but I have never seen it myself."

He ceased speaking with that far-off cadence in his voice with which he always ended a legend, and for a long time we both sat in silence listening to the rains that were still beating against the window.

The Sea-Serpent

There is one vice that is absolutely unknown to the red man; he was born without it, and amongst all the deplorable things he has learned from the white races, this, at least, he has never acquired. That is the vice of avarice. That the Indian looks upon greed of gain, miserliness, avariciousness, and wealth accumulated above the head of his poorer neighbour as one of the lowest degradations he can fall to, is perhaps more aptly illustrated in this legend than anything I could quote to demonstrate his horror of what he calls "the white man's unkindness."

In a very wide and varied experience with many tribes, I have yet to find even one instance of avarice, and I have encountered but one single case of a "stingy Indian," and this man was so marked amongst his fellows that at mention of his name his tribespeople jeered and would remark contemptuously that he was like a white man—hated to share his money and his possessions. All red races are born socialists, and most tribes carry out their communistic ideas to the letter. Amongst the Iroquois it is considered disgraceful to have food if your neighbour has none. To be a creditable member of the nation you must divide your possessions with your less fortunate fellows. I find it much the same amongst the Coast Indians, though they are less bitter in their hatred of the extremes of wealth and poverty than are the Eastern tribes. Still, the very fact that they have preserved this legend, in which they liken avarice to a slimy sea-serpent, shows the trend of their ideas; shows, too, that an Indian is an Indian, no matter what his tribe; shows that he cannot or will not hoard money; shows that his native morals demand that the spirit of greed must be strangled at all cost.

The chief and I had sat long over our luncheon. He had been talking of his trip to England and of the many curious things he had seen. At last, in an outburst of enthusiasm, he said: "I saw everything in the world—everything but a sea-serpent!"

"But there is no such thing as a sea-serpent," I laughed, "so you must have really seen everything in the world."

His face clouded; for a moment he sat in silence; then looking directly at me said, "Maybe none now, but long ago there was one here—in the Inlet."

"How long ago?" I asked.

"When first the white gold-hunters came," he replied. "Came with greedy, clutching fingers, greedy eyes, greedy hearts. The white men fought, murdered, starved, went mad with love of that gold far up the Fraser River. Tillicums were tillicums no more, brothers were foes, fathers and sons were enemies. Their love of the gold was a curse."

"Was it then the sea-serpent was seen?" I asked, perplexed with the problem of trying to connect the gold-seekers with such a monster.

"Yes, it was then, but——" he hesitated, then plunged into the assertion, "but you will not believe the story if you think there is no such thing as a sea-serpent."

"I shall believe whatever you tell me, Chief," I answered; "I am only too ready to believe. You know I come of a superstitious race, and all my association with the Palefaces has never yet robbed me of my birthright to believe strange traditions."

"You always understand," he said after a pause.

"It's my heart that understands," I remarked quietly.

He glanced up quickly, and with one of his all too few radiant smiles, he laughed.

"Yes, skookum tum-tum." Then without further hesitation he told the tradition, which, although not of ancient happening, is held in great reverence by his tribe. During its recital he sat with folded arms, leaning on the table, his head and shoulders bending eagerly towards me as I sat at the opposite side. It was the only time he ever talked to me when he did not use emphasizing gesticulations, but his hands never once lifted: his wonderful eyes alone gave expression to what he called "The Legend of the 'Salt-chuck Oluk'" (sea-serpent).

"Yes, it was during the first gold craze, and many of our young men went as guides to the whites far up the Fraser. When they returned they brought these tales of greed and murder back with them, and our old people and our women shook their heads and said evil would come of it. But all our young men, except one, returned as they went—kind to the poor, kind to those who were foodless, sharing whatever they had with their tillicums. But one, by name Shak-shak (The Hawk), came back with hoards of gold nuggets, chickimin,* everything; he was rich like the white men, and, like them, he kept it. He would count his chickimin, count his nuggets, gloat over them, toss them in his palms. He rested his head on them as he slept, he packed them about with him through the day. He loved them better than food, better than his tillicums, better than his life. The entire tribe arose. They said Shak-shak had the disease of greed; that to cure it he must give a great potlatch, divide his riches with the poorer ones, share them with the old, the sick, the foodless. But he jeered and laughed and told them No, and went on loving and gloating over his gold.

"Then the Sagalie Tyee spoke out of the sky and said, 'Shak-shak, you have made of yourself a loathsome thing; you will not listen to the cry of the hungry, to the call of the old and sick; you will not share your possessions; you have made of yourself an outcast from your tribe and disobeyed the ancient laws of your people. Now I will make of you a thing loathed and hated by all men, both white and red. You will have two heads, for your greed has two mouths

*Money.

to bite. One bites the poor, and one bites your own evil heart—and the fangs in these mouths are poison, poison that kills the hungry, and poison that kills your own manhood. Your evil heart will beat in the very centre of your foul body, and he that pierces it will kill the disease of greed forever from amongst his people.' And when the sun arose above the North Arm the next morning the tribespeople saw a gigantic sea-serpent stretched across the surface of the waters. One hideous head rested on the bluffs at Brockton Point, the other rested on a group of rocks just below Mission, at the western edge of North Vancouver. It you care to go there some day I will show you the hollow in one great stone where that head lay. The tribespeople were stunned with horror. They loathed the creature, they hated it, they feared it. Day after day it lay there, its monstrous heads lifted out of the waters, its mile-long body blocking all entrance from the Narrows, all outlet from the North Arm. The chiefs made council, the medicine men danced and chanted, but the salt-chuck oluk never moved. It could not move, for it was the hated totem of what now rules the white man's world—greed and love of chicki-min. No one can ever move the love of chicki-min from the white man's heart, no one can ever make him divide all with the poor. But after the chiefs and medicine men had done all in their power, and still the salt-chuck oluk lay across the waters, a handsome boy of sixteen approached them and reminded them of the words of the Sagalie Tyee, 'that he who pierced the monster's heart would kill the disease of greed forever amongst his people.'

" Let me try to find this evil heart, oh! great men of my tribe,' he cried. 'Let me war upon this creature; let me try to rid my people of this pestilence.'

"The boy was brave and very beautiful. His tribespeople called him the Tenas Tyee (Little Chief) and they loved him. Of all his wealth of fish and furs, of game and hykwa (large shell money) he gave to the boys who had none; he hunted food for the old people; he tanned skins and furs for those whose feet were feeble, whose eyes were fading, whose blood ran thin with age.

" 'Let him go!' cried the tribespeople. 'This unclean monster can only be overcome by cleanliness, this creature of greed can only be overthrown by generosity. Let him go!' The chiefs and the medicine men listened, then con-sented. 'Go,' they commanded, 'and fight this thing with your strongest weapons—cleanliness and generosity.'

"The Tenas Tyee turned to his mother. 'I

83

shall be gone four days,' he told her, 'and I shall swim all that time. I have tried all my life to be generous, but the people say I must be clean also to fight this unclean thing. While I am gone put fresh furs on my bed every day, even if I am not here to lie on them; if I know my bed, my body, and my heart are all clean I can overcome this serpent.'

" 'Your bed shall have fresh furs every morning,' his mother said simply.

"The Tenas Tyee then stripped himself and, with no clothing save a buckskin belt into which he thrust his hunting-knife, he flung his lithe young body into the sea. But at the end of four days he did not return. Sometimes his people could see him swimming far out in mid-channel, endeavouring to find the exact centre of the serpent, where lay its evil, selfish heart; but on the fifth morning they saw him rise out of the sea, climb to the summit of Brockton Point and greet the rising sun with outstretched arms. Weeks and months went by, still the Tenas Tyee would swim daily searching for that heart of greed; and each morning the sunrise glinted on his slender young copper-coloured body as he stood with outstretched arms at the tip of Brockton Point, greeting the coming day and then plunging from the summit into the sea.

"And at his home on the north shore his

mother dressed his bed with fresh furs each morning. The seasons drifted by, winter followed summer, summer followed winter. But it was four years before the Tenas Tyee found the centre of the great salt-chuck oluk and plunged his hunting-knife into its evil heart. In its death-agony it writhed through the Narrows, leaving a trail of blackness on the waters. Its huge body began to shrink, to shrivel; it became dwarfed and withered, until nothing but the bones of its back remained, and they, sea-bleached and lifeless, soon sank to the bed of the ocean leagues off from the rim of land. But as the Tenas Tyee swam homeward and his clean, young body crossed through the black stain left by the serpent, the waters became clear and blue and sparkling. He had overcome even the trail of the salt-chuck oluk.

"When at last he stood in the doorway of his home he said, 'My mother, I could not have killed the monster of greed amongst my people had you not helped me by keeping one place for me at home fresh and clean for my return.'

"She looked at him as only mothers look. 'Each day these four years, fresh furs have I laid for your bed. Sleep now, and rest, oh! my Tenas Tyee,' she said."

* * * *

85

The chief unfolded his arms, and his voice took another tone as he said, "What do you call that story—a legend?"

"The white people would call it an allegory," I answered. He shook his head.

"No savvy," he smiled.

I explained as simply as possible, and with his customary alertness he immediately understood. "That's right," he said. "That's what we say it means, we Squamish, that greed is evil and not clean, like the salt-chuck oluk. That it must be stamped out amongst our people, killed by cleanliness and generosity. The boy that overcame the serpent was both these things."

"What became of this splendid boy?" I asked.

"The Tenas Tyee? Oh! some of our old, old people say they sometimes see him now, standing on Brockton Point, his bare young arms outstretched to the rising sun," he replied.

"Have you ever seen him, Chief?" I questioned.

"No," he answered simply. But I have never heard such poignant regret as his wonderful voice crowded into that single word.

The Lost Island

"Yes," said my old tillicum, "we Indians have lost many things. We have lost our lands, our forests, our game, our fish; we have lost our ancient religion, our ancient dress; some of the younger people have even lost their fathers' language and the legends and traditions of their ancestors. We cannot call those old things back to us; they will never come again. We may travel many days up the mountain trails, and look in the silent places for them. They are not there. We may paddle many moons on the sea, but our canoes will never enter the channel that leads to the yesterdays of the Indian people. These things are lost, just like 'The Island of the North Arm.' They may be somewhere nearby, but no one can ever find them."

"But there are many islands up the North Arm," I asserted.

"Not the island we Indian people have sought for many tens of summers," he replied sorrowfully.

"Was it ever there?" I questioned.

"Yes, it was there," he said. "My grandsires and my great-grandsires saw it; but that was long ago. My father never saw it, though he spent many days in many years searching, always searching, for it. I am an old man myself, and I have never seen it, though from my youth I, too, have searched. Sometimes in the stillness of the nights I have paddled up in my canoe." Then, lowering his voice: "Twice I have seen its shadow: high rocky shores, reaching as high as the tree tops on the mainland, then tall pines and firs on its summit like a king's crown. As I paddled up the Arm one summer night, long ago, the shadow of these rocks and firs fell across my canoe, across my face, and across the waters beyond. I turned rapidly to look. There was no island there, nothing but a wide stretch of waters on both sides of me, and the moon almost directly overhead. Don't say it was the shore that shadowed me," he hastened, catching my thought. "The moon was above me; my canoe scarce made a shadow on the still waters. No, it was not the shore."

"Why do you search for it?" I lamented, thinking of the old dreams in my own life whose realization I have never attained.

"There is something on that island that I want. I shall look for it until I die, for it is there," he affirmed.

There was a long silence between us after that. I had learned to love silences when with my old tillicum, for they always led to a legend. After a time he began voluntarily:

"It was more than one hundred years ago. This great city of Vancouver was but the dream of the Sagalie Tyee (God) at that time. The dream had not yet come to the white man; only one great Indian medicine man knew that some day a great camp for Palefaces would lie between False Creek and the Inlet. This dream haunted him; it came to him night and day— when he was amid his people laughing and feasting, or when he was alone in the forest chanting his strange songs, beating his hollow drum, or shaking his wooden witch-rattle to gain more power to cure the sick and the dying of his tribe. For years this dream followed him. He grew to be an old, old man, yet always he could hear voices, strong and loud, as when they first spoke to him in his youth. and they would say: 'Between the two narrow strips of salt water the white men will camp—many hundreds of them, many thousands of them. The Indians will learn their ways, will live as they do, will become as they are. There will be no more great war dances, no more fights with other powerful tribes; it will be as if the Indians had lost all bravery, all courage, all confidence.' He hated the voices, he hated the dream; but all his power, all his big medicine, could not drive them away. He was the strongest man on all the North Pacific Coast. He was mighty and very tall, and his muscles were as those of Laloo, the timber wolf, when he is strongest to kill his prey. He could go for many days without food; he could fight the largest mountain lion; he could overthrow the fiercest grizzly bear; he could paddle against the wildest winds and ride the highest waves. He could meet his enemies and kill whole tribes single-handed. His strength, his courage, his power, his bravery, were those of a giant. He knew no fear; nothing in the sea, or in the forest, nothing in the earth or the sky, could conquer him. He was fearless, fearless. Only this haunting dream of the coming white man's camp he could not drive away; it was the one thing in life he had tried to kill and failed. It drove him from the feasting, drove him from the pleasant lodges, the fires, the dancing, the story-telling of his people in their camp by the water's edge, where the salmon thronged and the deer came down to drink of the mountain streams. He left the Indian village, chanting his wild songs as he went. Up through the mighty forests he climbed, through the trailless deep mosses and matted vines, up to the summit of what the white men call Grouse Mountain. For many days he camped there. He ate no food, he drank no water, but sat and sang his medicine songs through the dark hours and through the day. Before him—far beneath his feet—lay the narrow strip of land between the two salt waters. Then the Sagalie Tyee gave him the power to see far into the future. He looked across a hundred years, just as he looked across what you call the Inlet, and he saw mighty lodges built close together, hundreds and thousands of them; lodges of stone and wood, and long straight trails to divide them. He saw these trails thronging with Palefaces; he heard the sound of the white man's paddle-dip on the waters, for it is not silent like the Indian's; he saw the white man's trading posts, saw the fishing nets, heard his speech. Then the vision faded as gradually as it came. The narrow strip of land was his own forest once more.

" 'I am old,' he called, in his sorrow and his trouble for his people. 'I am old, oh, Sagalie

93

Tyee. Soon I shall die and go to the Happy Hunting Grounds of my fathers. Let not my strength die with me. Keep living for all time my courage, my bravery, my fearlessness. Keep them for my people that they may be strong enough to endure the white man's rule. Keep my strength living for them; hide it so that the Paleface may never find or see it.'

"Then he came down from the summit of Grouse Mountain. Still chanting his medicine songs he entered his canoe, and paddled through the colours of the setting sun far up the North Arm. When night fell he came to an island with misty shores of great grey rock; on its summit tall pines and firs circled like a king's crown. As he neared it he felt all his strength, his courage, his fearlessness, leaving him; he could see these things drift from him on to the island. They were as the clouds that rest on the mountains, grey-white and half transparent. Weak as a woman he paddled back to the Indian village; he told them to go and search for 'The Island,' where they would find all his courage, his fearlessness and his strength, living, living forever. He slept then, but—in the morning he did not awake. Since then our young men and our old have searched for 'The Island.' It is there somewhere, up some lost channel, but we cannot find it. When we do, we will get back all the courage and bravery we had before the white man came, for the great medicine man said those things never die—they live for one's children and grandchildren."

His voice ceased. My whole heart went out to him in his longing for the lost island. I thought of all the splendid courage I knew him to possess, so made answer: "But you say that the shadow of this island has fallen upon you; is it not so, tillicum?"

"Yes," he said half-mournfully. "But only the shadow."

Point Grey

"Have you ever sailed around Point Grey?"
asked a young Squamish tillicum of mine who
often comes to see me, to share a cup of tea and
a taste of muck-a-muck, that otherwise I should
eat in solitude.

"No," I admitted, I had not had that pleasure,
for I did not know the uncertain waters of
English Bay sufficiently well to venture about
its headlands in my frail canoe.

"Some day, perhaps next summer, I'll take
you there in a sailboat, and show you the big

97

rock at the southwest of the Point. It is a strange rock; we Indian people call it Homolsom."

"What an odd name," I commented. "Is it a Squamish word?—it does not sound to me like one."

"It is not altogether Squamish, but half Fraser River language. The Point was the dividing line between the grounds and waters of the two tribes, so they agreed to make the name 'Homolsom' from the two languages."

I suggested more tea, and, as he sipped it, he told me the legend that few of the younger Indians know. That he believes the story himself is beyond question, for many times he admitted having tested the virtues of this rock, and it had never once failed him. All people that have to do with water craft are superstitious about some things, and I freely acknowledge that times innumerable I have "whistled up" a wind when dead calm threatened, or stuck a jack-knife in the mast, and afterwards watched with great contentment the idle sail fill, and the canoe pull out to a light breeze. So, perhaps, I am prejudiced in favour of this legend of Homolsom Rock, for it strikes a very responsive chord in that portion of my heart that has always throbbed for the sea.

"You know," began my young tillicum, "that only waters unspoiled by human hands can be of any benefit. One gains no strength by swimming in any waters heated or boiled by fires that men build. To grow strong and wise one must swim in the natural rivers, the mountain torrents, the sea, just as the Sagalie Tyee made them. Their virtues die when human beings try to improve them by heating or distilling, or placing even tea in them, and so—what makes Homolsom Rock so full of 'good medicine' is that the waters that wash up about it are straight from the sea, made by the hand of the Great Tyee, and unspoiled by the hand of man.

"It was not always there, that great rock, drawing its strength and its wonderful power from the seas, for it, too, was once a Great Tyee, who ruled a mighty tract of waters. He was god of all the waters that wash the coast, of the Gulf of Georgia, of Puget Sound, of the Straits of Juan de Fuca, of the waters that beat against even the west coast of Vancouver Island, and of all the channels that cut between the Charlotte Islands. He was Tyee of the West Wind, and his storms and tempests were so mighty that the Sagalie Tyee Himself could not control the havoc that he created. He warred upon all fishing craft, he demolished canoes and sent men to graves in the sea. He uprooted forests and drove the surf on shore heavy with wreckage of despoiled trees and with beaten and bruised fish.

He did all this to reveal his powers, for he was cruel and hard of heart, and he would laugh and defy the Sagalie Tyee, and looking up to the sky he would call, 'See how powerful I am, how mighty, how strong; I am as great as you.'

"It was at this time that the Sagalie Tyee in the persons of the Four Men came in the great canoe up over the rim of the Pacific, in that age thousands of years ago when they turned the evil into stone, and the kindly into trees.

" 'Now,' said the god of the West Wind, 'I can show how great I am. I shall blow a tempest that these men may not land on my coast. They shall not ride my seas and sounds and channels in safety. I shall wreck them and send their bodies into the great deeps, and I shall be Sagalie Tyee in their place and ruler of all the world.' So the god of the West Wind blew forth his tempests. The waves arose mountain high, the seas lashed and thundered along the shores. The roar of his mighty breath could be heard wrenching giant limbs from the forest trees, whistling down the canyons and dealing death and destruction for leagues and leagues along the coast. But the canoe containing the Four Men rode upright through all the heights and hollows of the seething ocean. No curling crest or sullen depth could wreck that magic craft, for the hearts it bore were filled with kindness for the human race, and kindness cannot die.

"It was all rock and dense forest, and un-peopled; only wild animals and sea birds sought the shelter it provided from the terrors of the West Wind; but he drove them out in sullen anger, and made on this strip of land his last stand against the Four Men. The Paleface calls the place Point Grey, but the Indians yet speak of it as 'The Battle Ground of the West Wind.' All his mighty forces he now brought to bear against the oncoming canoe; he swept great hurricanes about the stony ledges; he caused the sea to beat and swirl in tempestuous fury along its narrow fastnesses, but the canoe came nearer and nearer, invincible as those shores, and stronger than death itself. As the bow touched the land the Four Men arose and commanded the West Wind to cease his war cry and, mighty though he had been, his voice trembled and sobbed itself into a gentle breeze, then fell to a whispering note, then faded into exquisite silence.

" 'Oh, you evil one with the unkind heart,' cried the Four Men, 'you have been too great a god for even the Sagalie Tyee to obliterate you forever, but you shall live on, live now to serve, not to hinder mankind. You shall turn into stone where you now stand, and you shall rise only as men wish you to. Your life from this day shall be for the good of man, for when the fisherman's sails are idle and his lodge is leagues away you shall fill those sails and blow his craft free, in whatever direction he desires. You shall stand where you are through all the thousands upon thousands of years to come, and he who touches you with his paddle-blade shall have his desire of a breeze to carry him home.' "

My young tillicum had finished his tradition, and his great solemn eyes regarded me half-wistfully.

"I wish you could see Homolsom Rock," he said. "For that is he who was once the Tyee of the West Wind."

"Were you ever becalmed around Point Grey?" I asked irrelevantly.

"Often," he replied. "But I paddle up to the rock and touch it with the tip of my paddle-blade, and no matter which way I want to go the wind will blow free for me, if I wait a little while."

"I suppose your people all do this?" I replied.

"Yes, all of them," he answered. "They have done it for hundreds of years. You see the power in it is just as great now as at first, for the rock feeds every day on the unspoiled sea that the Sagalie Tyee made."

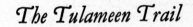

The Tulameen Trail

Did you ever "holiday" through the valley lands of the Dry Belt? Ever spend days and days in a swinging, swaying coach, behind a four-in-hand, when "Curly" or "Nicola Ned" held the ribbons, and tooled his knowing little leaders and wheelers down those horrifying mountain trails that wind like russet skeins of cobweb through the heights and depths of the Okanagan, the Nicola and the Similkameen countries? If so, you have listened to the call of the Skookum Chuck, as the Chinook speakers call the rollicking, tumbling streams that sing their way through the canyons with a music so dulcet, so insistent, that for many moons the echo of it lingers in your listening ears, and you will, through all the years to come, hear the voices of those mountain rivers calling you to return.

But the most haunting of all the melodies is the warbling laughter of the Tulameen; its delicate note is far more powerful, more far-reaching than the throaty thunders of Niagara. That is why the Indians of the Nicola country still cling to their old-time story that the Tulameen carries the spirit of a young girl enmeshed in the wonders of its winding course; a spirit that can never free itself from the canyons, to rise above the heights and follow its fellows to the Happy Hunting Grounds, but which is contented to entwine its laughter, its sobs, its lonely whispers, its still lonelier call for companionship, with the wild music of the waters that sing forever beneath the western stars.

As your horses plod up and up the almost perpendicular trail that leads out of the Nicola Valley to the summit, a paradise of beauty outspreads at your feet; the colour is indescribable in words, the atmosphere thrills you. Youth and the pulse of rioting blood are yours again until, as you near the heights, you become strangely calmed by the voiceless silence of it all, a silence so holy that it seems the whole world about you is swinging its censer before an altar in some dim remote cathedral! The choir voices of the Tulameen are yet very far away across the summit, but the heights of the Nicola are the silent prayer that holds the human soul before the first great chords swell down from the organ loft. In this first long climb up miles and miles of trail, even the staccato of the driver's long black-snake whip is hushed. He lets his animals pick their own sure-footed way, but once across the summit he gathers the reins in his steely fingers, gives a low, quick whistle, the whiplash curls about the ears of the leaders and the plunge down the dip of the mountain begins. Every foot of the way is done at a gallop. The coach rocks and swings as it dashes through a trail rough-hewn from the heart of the forest; at times the angles are so abrupt that you cannot see the heads of the leaders as they swing around the grey crags that almost scrape the tires on the left, while within a foot of the rim of the trail the right wheels whirl along the edge of a yawning canyon. The rhythm of the hoof-beats, the recurrent low whistle and crack of the whip-lash, the occasional rattle of pebbles showering down to the depths, loosened by rioting wheels, have broken the sacred silence. Yet above all those nearby sounds there seems to be an indistinct murmur, which grows sweeter, more musical, as you gain the base of the mountains, where it rises above all harsher notes. It is the voice of the restless Tulameen as it dances and laughs through the rocky throat of the canyon, three hundred feet below. Then, following the song, comes a glimpse of the river itself—white garmented in the film of its countless rapids, its showers of waterfalls. It is as beautiful to look at as to listen to, and it is here, where the trail winds about and above it for leagues, that the Indians say it caught the spirit of the maiden that is still interlaced in its loveliness.

It was in one of the terrible battles that raged between the valley tribes before the white man's footprints were seen along these trails. None can now tell the cause of this warfare, but the supposition is that it was merely for tribal supremacy—that primeval instinct that assails the savage in both man and beast, that drives the hill men to bloodshed and the leaders of buffalo herds to conflict. It is the greed to rule; the one barbarous instinct that civilization has never yet been able to eradicate from armed nations. This war of the tribes of the valley lands was of years in duration; men fought and women mourned, and children wept, as all have done since time began. It seemed an unequal battle, for the old experienced war-tried chief and his two astute sons were pitted against a single young Tulameen brave. Both factors had their loyal followers, both were indomitable as to courage and bravery, both were determined and ambitious, both were skilled fighters.

But on the older man's side were experience and two other wary, strategic brains to help him, while on the younger was but the advantage of splendid youth and unconquerable persistence. But at every pitched battle, at every skirmish, at every single-handed conflict the younger man gained little by little, the older man lost step by step. The experience of age was gradually but inevitably giving way to the strength and enthusiasm of youth. Then one day they met face to face and alone—the old war-scarred chief, the young battle-inspired brave. It was an unequal combat, and at the close of a brief but violent struggle the younger had brought the older to his knees. Standing over him with up-poised knife the Tulameen brave laughed sneeringly, and said:

"Would you, my enemy, have this victory as your own? If so, I give it to you; but in

return for my submission I demand of you—
your daughter."

For an instant the old chief looked in won-
derment at his conqueror; he thought of his
daughter only as a child who played about the
forest trails or sat obediently beside her mother
in the lodge, stitching her little moccasins or
weaving her little baskets.

"My daughter!" he answered sternly. "My
daughter—who is barely out of her own cradle
basket—give her to you, whose hands are blood-
dyed with the killing of a score of my tribe?
You ask for this thing?"

"I do not ask it," replied the young brave.
"I demand it; I have seen the girl and I shall
have her."

The old chief sprang to his feet and spat
out his refusal. "Keep your victory, and I keep
my girl-child," though he knew he was not
only defying his enemy, but defying death as
well.

The Tulameen laughed lightly, easily. "I shall
not kill the sire of my wife," he taunted. "One
more battle must we have, but your girl-child
will come to me."

Then he took his victorious way up the
trail, while the old chief walked with slow and
springless step down into the canyon.

The next morning the chief's daughter was

loitering along the heights, listening to the singing river, and sometimes leaning over the precipice to watch its curling eddies and dancing waterfalls. Suddenly she heard a slight rustle, as though some passing bird's wing had clipt the air. Then at her feet there fell a slender, delicately shaped arrow. It fell with spent force, and her Indian woodcraft told her it had been shot to her, not at her. She started like a wild animal. Then her quick eye caught the outline of a handsome, erect figure that stood on the heights across the river. She did not know him as her father's enemy. She only saw him to be young, stalwart and of extraordinary, manly beauty. The spirit of youth and of a certain savage coquetry awoke within her. Quickly she fitted one of her own dainty arrows to the bow string and sent it winging across the narrow canyon; it fell, spent, at his feet, and he knew she had shot it to him, not at him.

Next morning, woman-like, she crept noiselessly to the brink of the heights. Would she see him again—that handsome brave? Would he speed another arrow to her? She had not yet emerged from the tangle of forest before it fell, its faint-winged flight heralding its coming. Near the feathered end was tied a tassel of beautiful ermine tails. She took from her wrist a string of shell beads, fastened it to one of her little arrows and winged it across the canyon, as yesterday.

The following morning before leaving the lodge she fastened the tassel of ermine tails in her straight, black hair. Would he see them? But no arrow fell at her feet that day, but a dearer message was there on the brink of the precipice. He himself awaited her coming—he who had never left her thoughts since that first arrow came to her from his bow-string. His eyes burned with warm fires, as she approached, but his lips said simply: "I have crossed the Tulameen River." Together they stood, side by side, and looked down at the depths before them, watching in silence the little torrent rollicking and roystering over its boulders and crags.

"That is my country," he said, looking across the river. "This is the country of your father, and of your brothers; they are my enemies. I return to my own shore tonight. Will you come with me?"

She looked up into his handsome young face. So this was her father's foe—the dreaded Tulameen!

"Will you come?" he repeated.

"I will come," she whispered.

It was in the dark of the moon and through the kindly night he led her far up the rocky shores to the narrow belt of quiet waters, where they crossed in silence into his own country. A week, a month, a long golden summer, slipped by, but the insulted old chief and his enraged sons failed to find her.

Then one morning as the lovers walked together on the heights above the far upper reaches of the river, even the ever-watchful eyes of the Tulameen failed to detect the lurking enemy. Across the narrow canyon crouched and crept the two outwitted brothers of the girl-wife at his side; their arrows were on their bow-strings, their hearts on fire with hatred and vengeance. Like two evil-winged birds of prey those arrows sped across the laughing river, but before they found their mark in the breast of the victorious Tulameen the girl had unconsciously stepped before him. With a little sigh, she slipped into his arms, her brothers' arrows buried into her soft, brown flesh.

It was many a moon before his avenging hand succeeded in slaying the old chief and those two hated sons of his. But when this was finally done the handsome young Tulameen left his people, his tribe, his country, and went into the far north. "For," he said, as he sang

113

his farewell war song, "my heart lies dead in the Tulameen River."

*   *   *   *

But the spirit of his girl-wife still sings through the canyon, its song blending with the music of that sweetest-voiced river in all the great valleys of the Dry Belt. That is why this laughter, the sobbing murmur of the beautiful Tulameen will haunt for evermore the ear that has once listened to its song.

The Grey Archway

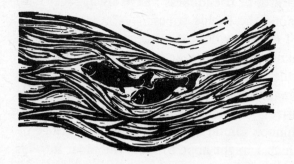

The steamer, like a huge shuttle, wove in and out among the countless small islands; its long trailing scarf of grey smoke hung heavily along the uncertain shores, casting a shadow over the pearly waters of the Pacific, which swung lazily from rock to rock in indescribable beauty.

After dinner I wandered astern with the traveller's ever-present hope of seeing the beauties of a typical Northern sunset, and by some happy chance I placed my deck stool near an old tillicum, who was leaning on the rail, his pipe between his thin curved lips, his brown hands clasped idly, his sombre eyes looking far out to sea, as though they searched the future—or was it that they were seeing the past?

"Kla-how-ya, tillicum!" I greeted.

He glanced round, and half smiled.

117

"Kla-how-ya, tillicum!" he replied, with the warmth of friendliness I have always met with among the Pacific tribes.

I drew my deck stool nearer to him, and he acknowledged the action with another half-smile, but did not stir from his entrenchment, remaining as if hedged about with an inviolable fortress of exclusiveness. Yet I knew that my Chinook salutation would be a draw-bridge by which I might hope to cross the moat into his castle of silence.

Indian-like, he took his time before continuing the acquaintance. Then he began in most excellent English:

"You do not know these Northern waters?"

I shook my head.

After many moments he leaned forwards, looking along the curve of the deck, up the channels and narrows we were threading, to a broad strip of waters off the port bow. Then he pointed with that peculiar, thoroughly Indian gesture of the palm uppermost.

"Do you see it—over there? The small island? It rests on the edge of the water, like a grey gull."

It took my unaccustomed eyes some moments to discern it; then all at once I caught its outline, veiled in the mists of distance—grey, cobwebby, dreamy.

118

"Yes," I replied, "I see it now. You will tell me of it—tillicum?"

He gave a swift glance at my dark skin, then nodded. "You are one of us," he said, with evidently no thought of a possible contradiction. "And you will understand, or I should not tell you. You will not smile at the story, for you are one of us."

"I am one of you, and I shall understand," I answered.

It was a full half-hour before we neared the island, yet neither of us spoke during that time; then, as the "grey gull" shaped itself into rock and tree and crag, I noticed in the very centre a stupendous pile of stone lifting itself skyward, without fissure or cleft; but a peculiar haziness about the base made me peer narrowly to catch the perfect outline.

"It is the 'Grey Archway,' " he explained simply.

Only then did I grasp the singular formation before us; the rock itself was a perfect archway, through which we could see the placid Pacific shimmering in the growing colours of the coming sunset at the opposite rim of the island.

"What a remarkable whim of Nature!" I exclaimed, but his brown hand was laid in a contradictory grasp on my arm, and he snatched up my comment almost with impatience.

"No, it was not Nature," he said. "That is the reason I say you will understand—you are one of us—you will know what I tell you is true. The Great Tyee did not make that archway, it was—" here his voice lowered—"it was magic, red man's medicine and magic—you savvy?"

"Yes," I said. "Tell me, for I—savvy."

"Long time ago," he began, stumbling into a half-broken English language because, I think, of the atmosphere and environment, "long before you were born, or your father, or grandfather, or even his father, this strange thing happened. It is a story for women to hear, to remember. Women are the future mothers of the tribe, and we of the Pacific Coast hold such in high regard, in great reverence. The women who are mothers—o-ho!—they are the important ones, we say. Warriors, fighters, brave men, fearless daughters, owe their qualities to these mothers—eh, is it not always so?"

I nodded silently. The island was swinging nearer to us, the "Grey Archway" loomed almost above us, the mysticism crowded close, it enveloped me, caressed me, appealed to me.

"And?" I hinted.

"And," he proceeded, "this 'Grey Archway'

is a story of mothers, of magic, of witchcraft, of warriors, of—love."

An Indian rarely uses the word "love," and when he does it expresses every quality, every attribute, every intensity, emotion and passion embraced in those four little letters. Surely this was an exceptional story I was to hear.

I did not answer, only looked across the pulsing waters towards the "Grey Archway," which the sinking sun was touching with soft pastels, tints one could give no name to, beauties impossible to describe.

"You have not heard of Yaada?" he questioned. Then fortunately he continued without waiting for a reply. He well knew that I had never heard of Yaada, so why not begin without preliminary to tell me of her?—so—

"Yaada was the loveliest daughter of the Haida tribe. Young braves from all the islands, from the mainland, from the upper Skeena country came, hoping to carry her to their faroff lodges, but they always returned alone. She was the most desired of all the island maidens, beautiful, brave, modest, the daughter of her own mother.

"But there was a great man, a very great man—a medicine man, skilful, powerful, influential, old, deplorably old, and very, very rich; he said, 'Yaada shall be my wife,' And there was a young fisherman, handsome, loyal, boyish, poor, oh! very poor, and gloriously young, and he, too, said, 'Yaada shall be my wife.'

"But Yaada's mother sat apart and thought and dreamed, as mothers will. She said to herself, 'The great medicine man has power, has vast riches, and wonderful magic, why not give her to him? But Ulka has the boy's heart, the boy's beauty, he is very brave, very strong; why not give her to him?'

"But the laws of the great Haida tribe prevailed. Its wise men said, 'Give the girl to the greatest man, give her to the most powerful, the richest. The man of magic must have his choice.'

"But at this the mother's heart grew as wax in the summer sunshine—it is a strange quality that mothers' hearts are made of! 'Give her to the best man—the man her heart holds highest,' said this Haida mother.

"Then Yaada spoke: 'I am the daughter of my tribe; I would judge of men by their excellence. He who proves most worthy I shall marry; it is not riches that make a good husband; it is not beauty that makes a good father for one's children. Let me and my tribe see some proof of the excellence of these two men—then, only, shall I choose who is to be the father of my children. Let us have a trial of their skill; let them show me how evil or how beautiful is the inside of their hearts. Let each of them throw a stone with some intent, some purpose in their hearts. He who makes the noblest mark may call me wife.'

" 'Alas! Alas!' wailed the Haida mother. 'This casting of stones does not show worth. It but shows prowess.'

" 'But I have implored the Sagalie Tyee of my father, and of his fathers before him, to help me to judge between them by this means,' said the girl. 'So they must cast the stones. In this way only shall I see their innermost hearts.'

"The medicine man never looked so old as at that moment; so hopelessly old, so wrinkled, so palsied: he was no mate for Yaada. Ulka never looked so god-like in his young beauty, so gloriously young, so courageous. The girl, looking at him, loved him—almost was she placing her hand in his, but the spirit of her forefathers halted her. She had spoken the word—she must abide by it. 'Throw!' she commanded.

"Into his shrivelled fingers the great medicine man took a small, round stone, chanting strange words of magic all the while; his greedy eyes were on the girl, his greedy thoughts about her.

"Into his strong, young fingers Ulka took a

smooth, flat stone; his handsome eyes were lowered in boyish modesty, his thoughts were worshipping her. The great medicine man cast his missile first; it swept through the air like a shaft of lightning, striking the great rock with a force that shattered it. At the touch of that stone the 'Grey Archway' opened and has remained open to this day.

" 'Oh, wonderful power and magic!' clamoured the entire tribe. 'The very rocks do his bidding.'

"But Yaada stood with eyes that burned in agony. Ulka could never command such magic —she knew it. But at her side Ulka was standing erect, tall, slender and beautiful, but just as he cast his missile the evil voice of the old medicine man began a still more evil incantation. He fixed his poisonous eyes on the younger man, eyes with hideous magic in their depths —ill-omened and enchanted with 'bad medicine.' The stone left Ulka's fingers; for a second it flew forth in a straight line, then as the evil voice of the old man grew louder in its incantations the stone curved. Magic had waylaid the strong arm of the young brave. The stone poised an instant above the forehead of Yaada's mother, then dropped with the weight of many mountains, and the last long sleep fell upon her.

" 'Slayer of my mother' stormed the girl, her suffering eyes fixed upon the medicine man. 'Oh, I now see your black heart through your black magic. Through good magic you cut the 'Grey Archway,' but your evil magic you used upon young Ulka. I saw your wicked eyes upon him; I heard your wicked incantations; I know your wicked heart. You used your heartless magic in hope of winning me—in hope of making him an outcast of the tribe. You cared not for my sorrowing heart, my motherless life to come.' Then, turning to the tribe, she demanded: 'Who of you saw his evil eyes fixed on Ulka? Who of you heard his evil song?'

" 'I,' and 'I,' and 'I,' came voice after voice.

" 'The very air is poisoned that we breathe about him,' they shouted. 'The young man is blameless, his heart is as the sun, but the man who has used his evil magic has a heart black and cold as the hours before the dawn.'

"Then Yaada's voice arose in a strange, sweet, sorrowful chant:

My feet shall walk no more upon this island,
  With its great, Grey Archway.
My mother sleeps forever on this island,
  With its great, Grey Archway.
My heart would break without her on this island,
  With its great, Grey Archway.

My life was of her life upon this island,
  With its great, Grey Archway.
My mother's soul has wandered from this island,
  With its great, Grey Archway.
My feet must follow hers beyond this island,
  With its great, Grey Archway.

"As Yaada chanted and wailed her farewell, she moved slowly towards the edge of the cliff. On its brink she hovered a moment with outstretched arms, as a sea gull poises on its weight—then she called:

" 'Ulka, my Ulka! Your hand is innocent of wrong; it was the evil magic of your rival that slew my mother. I must go to her; even you cannot keep me here; will you stay, or come with me? Oh! my Ulka!'

"The slender, gloriously young boy sprang towards her; their hands closed one within the other; for a second they poised on the brink of the rocks, radiant as stars; then together they plunged into the sea."

*   *   *   *

The legend was ended. Long ago we had passed the island with its "Grey Archway"; it was melting into the twilight, far astern.

As I brooded over this strange tale of a daughter's devotion, I watched the sea and sky for something that would give me a clue to the inevitable sequel that the tillicum, like all his race, was surely withholding until the opportune moment.

Something flashed through the darkening waters not a stone's throw from the steamer. I leaned forwards, watching it intently. Two silvery fish were making a succession of little leaps and plunges along the surface of the sea, their bodies catching the last tints of sunset, like flashing jewels. I looked at the tillicum quickly. He was watching me—a world of anxiety in his half-mournful eyes.

"And those two silvery fish?" I questioned.

He smiled. The anxious look vanished. "I was right," he said; "you do know us and our ways, for you are one of us. Yes, those fish are seen only in these waters; there are never but two of them. They are Yaada and her mate seeking for the soul of the Haida woman—her mother."

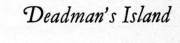
Deadman's Island

It is dusk on the Lost Lagoon,
And we two dreaming the dusk away,
Beneath the drift of a twilight grey—
Beneath the drowse of an ending day
And the curve of a golden moon.

It is dark in the Lost Lagoon,
And gone are the depths of haunting blue,
The grouping gulls, and the old canoe,
The singing firs, and the dusk and—you,
And gone is the golden moon.

O! lure of the Lost Lagoon—
I dream tonight that my paddle blurs
The purple shade where the seaweed stirs—
I hear the call of the singing firs
In the hush of the golden moon.

For many minutes we stood silently, leaning on the western rail of the bridge as we watched the sun set across that beautiful little basin of water known as Coal Harbour. I have always resented that jarring, unattractive name, for years ago, when I first plied paddle across the gunwale of a light little canoe, and idled about its margin, I named the sheltered little cove the Lost Lagoon. This was just to please my own fancy, for as that perfect summer month drifted on, the ever-restless tides left the harbour devoid of water at my favourite canoeing hour, and my pet idling place was lost for many days—hence my fancy to call it the Lost Lagoon. But the chief, Indian-like, immediately adopted the name, at least when he spoke of the place to me, and as we watched the sun slip behind the rim of firs, he expressed the wish that his dugout were here instead of lying beached at the farther side of the park.

"If canoe was here, you and I we paddle close to shores all 'round your Lost Lagoon: we make track just like half moon. Then we paddle under this bridge, and go channel between Deadman's Island and park. Then 'round where cannon speak time at nine o'clock. Then 'cross Inlet to Indian side of Narrows."

I turned to look eastwards, following in fancy the course he had sketched; the waters were

130

still as the footstep of the oncoming twilight and, floating in a pool of soft purple, Deadman's Island rested like a large circle of candle moss.

"Have you ever been on it?" he asked as he caught my gaze centring on the irregular outline of the island pines.

"I have prowled the length and depth of it," I told him. "Climbed over every rock on its shores, crept under every tangled growth of its interior, explored its overgrown trails, and more than once nearly got lost in its very heart."

"Yes," he half-laughed, "it pretty wild; not much good for anything."

"People seem to think it valuable," I said. "There is a lot of litigation—of fighting going on now about it."

"Oh! that the way always," he said as though speaking of a long-accepted fact. "Always fight over that place. Hundreds of years ago they fight about it; Indian people; they say hundreds of years to come everybody will still fight—never be settled what that place is, who it belong to, who has right to it. No, never settle. Deadman's Island always mean fight for someone."

"So the Indians fought amongst themselves about it?" I remarked, seemingly without guile, although my ears tingled for the legend I knew was coming.

"Fought like lynx at close quarters," he answered. "Fought, killed each other, until the island ran with blood redder than that sunset, and the sea water about it was stained flame colour—it was then, my people say, that the scarlet fire-flower was first seen growing along this coast."

"It is a beautiful colour—the fire-flower," I said.

"It should be fine colour, for it was born and grew from the hearts of fine tribespeople— very fine people," he emphasized.

We crossed to the eastern rail of the bridge, and stood watching the deep shadows that gathered slowly and silently about the island; I have seldom looked upon anything more peaceful.

The chief sighed. "We have no such men now, no fighters like those men, no hearts, no courage like theirs. But I tell you the story; you understand it then. Now all peace; tonight all good tillicums; even dead man's spirit does not fight now, but long time after it happen those spirits fought."

"And the legend?" I ventured.

"Oh! yes," he replied, as if suddenly returning to the present from out a far country in the realm of time. "Indian people, they call it the 'Legend of the Island of Dead Men.'

"There was war everywhere. Fierce tribes from the northern coast, savage tribes from the South, all met here and battled and raided, burned and captured, tortured and killed their enemies. The forests smoked with camp fires, the Narrows were choked with war canoes, and the Sagalie Tyee—He who is a man of peace—turned His face away from His Indian children. About this island there was dispute and contention. The medicine men from the North claimed it as their chanting ground. The medicine men from the South laid equal claim to it. Each wanted it as the stronghold of their witchcraft, their magic. Great bands of these medicine men met on the small space, using every sorcery in their power to drive their opponents away. The witch doctors of the North made their camp on the northern rim of the island; those from the South settled along the southern edge, looking towards what is now the great city of Vancouver. Both factions danced, chanted, burned their magic powders, built their magic fires, beat their magic rattles, but neither would give way, yet neither conquered. About them, on the waters, on the mainlands, raged the warfare of their respective tribes—the Sagalie Tyee had forgotten His Indian children.

"After many months, the warriors on both sides weakened. They said the incantations of the rival medicine men were bewitching them, were making their hearts like children's, and their arms nerveless as women's. So friend and foe arose as one man and drove the medicine men from the island, hounded them down the Inlet, herded them through the Narrows and banished them out to sea, where they took refuge on one of the outer islands of the gulf. Then the tribes once more fell upon each other in battle.

"The warrior blood of the North will always conquer. They are the stronger, bolder, more alert, more keen. The snows and the ice of their country make swifter pulse than the sleepy suns of the South can awake in a man; their muscles are of sterner stuff, their endurance greater. Yes, the northern tribes will always be victors.* But the craft and the strategy of the southern tribes are hard things to battle against. While those of the North followed the medicine men farther out to sea to make

* Note.—It would almost seem that the chief knew that wonderful poem of "The Khan's," "The Men of the Northern Zone," wherein he says :

> If ever a Northman lost a throne
> Did the conqueror come from the South?
> Nay, the North shall ever be free . . . etc.

sure of their banishment, those from the South returned under cover of night and seized the women and children and the old, enfeebled men in their enemy's camp, transported them all to the Island of Dead Men, and there held them as captives. Their war canoes circled the island like a fortification, through which drifted the sobs of the imprisoned women, the mutterings of the aged men, the wail of little children.

"Again and again the men of the North assailed that circle of canoes, and again and again were repulsed. The air was thick with poisoned arrows, the water stained with blood. But day by day the circle of southern canoes grew thinner and thinner; the northern arrows were telling, and truer of aim. Canoes drifted everywhere, empty, or worse still, manned only by dead men. The pick of the southern warriors had already fallen, when their greatest Tyee mounted a large rock on the eastern shore. Brave and unmindful of a thousand weapons aimed at his heart, he uplifted his hand, palm outwards—the signal for conference. Instantly every northern arrow was lowered, and every northern ear listened for his words.

" 'Oh! men of the Upper Coast,' he said, 'you are more numerous than we are; your tribe is larger; your endurance greater. We are growing hungry, we are growing less in numbers. Our captives—your women and children and old men—have lessened, too, our stores of food. If you refuse our terms we will yet fight to the finish. Tomorrow we will kill all our captives before your eyes, for we can feed them no longer, or you can have your wives, your mothers, your fathers, your children, by giving us for each and every one of them one of your best and bravest young warriors, who will consent to suffer death in their stead. Speak! You have your choice.'

"In the northern canoes scores and scores of young warriors leapt to their feet. The air was filled with glad cries, with exultant shouts. The whole world seemed to ring with the voices of those young men who called loudly, with glorious courage:

" 'Take me, but give me back my old father.'

" 'Take me, but spare to my tribe my little sister.'

" 'Take me, but release my wife and boy-baby.'

"So the compact was made. Two hundred heroic, magnificent young men paddled up to the island, broke through the fortifying circle of canoes and stepped ashore. They flaunted their eagle plumes with the spirit and boldness of young gods. Their shoulders were erect, their step was firm, their hearts strong. Into their canoes they crowded the two hundred captives. Once more their women sobbed, their old men muttered, their children wailed, but those young copper-coloured gods never flinched, never faltered. Their weak and their feeble were saved. What mattered to them such a little thing as death?

"The released captives were quickly surrounded by their own people, but the flower of their splendid nation was in the hands of their enemies, those valorous young men who thought so little of life that they willingly, gladly laid it down to serve and to save those they loved and cared for. Amongst them were war-tried warriors who had fought fifty battles, and boys not yet full grown, who were drawing a bow string for the first time, but their hearts, their courage, their self-sacrifice were as one.

"Out before a long file of southern warriors they stood. Their chins uplifted, their eyes defiant, their breasts bared. Each leaned forwards and laid his weapons at his feet, then stood erect, with empty hands, and laughed forth his challenge to death. A thousand arrows ripped the air, two hundred gallant northern throats flung forth a death cry exultant, triumphant as conquering kings—then two hundred fearless northern hearts ceased to beat.

"But in the morning the southern tribes

found the spot where they fell peopled with flaming fire-flowers. Dread terror seized upon them. They abandoned the island, and when night again shrouded them they manned their canoes and noiselessly slipped through the Narrows, turned their bows southwards and this coast line knew them no more."

"What glorious men," I half-whispered as the chief concluded the strange legend.

"Yes, men!" he echoed. "The white people call it Deadman's Island. That is their way; but we of the Squamish call it The Island of Dead Men."

The clustering pines and the outlines of the island's margin were now dusky and indistinct. Peace, peace lay over the waters, and the purple of the summer twilight had turned to grey, but I knew that in the depths of the undergrowth on Deadman's Island there blossomed a flower of flaming beauty; its colours were veiled in the coming nightfall, but somewhere down in the sanctuary of its petals pulsed the heart's blood of many and valiant men.

A Squamish Legend of Napoleon

Holding an important place among the majority of curious tales held in veneration by the Coast tribes are those of the sea-serpent. The monster appears and reappears with almost monotonous frequency in connection with history, traditions, legends, and superstitions; but perhaps the most wonderful part it ever played was in the great drama that held the stage of Europe, and incidentally all the world during the stormy days of the first Napoleon.

Throughout Canada I have never failed to find an amazing knowledge of Napoleon Bonaparte amongst the very old and "uncivilized" Indians. Perhaps they may be unfamiliar with every other historical character from Adam down, but they will all tell you they have heard of the "Great French Fighter," as they call the wonderful little Corsican.

Whether this knowledge was obtained

through the fact that our earliest settlers and pioneers were French, or whether Napoleon's almost magical fighting career attracted the Indian mind to the exclusion of lesser warriors, I have never yet decided. But the fact remains that the Indians of our generation are not as familiar with Bonaparte's name as were their fathers and grandfathers, so either the predominance of English-speaking settlers or the thinning of their ancient war-loving blood by modern civilization and peaceful times, must one or the other account for the younger Indian's ignorance of the Emperor of the French.

In telling me the legend of The Lost Talisman, my good tillicum, the late Chief Capilano, began the story with the almost amazing question: Had I ever heard of Napoleon Bonaparte? It was some moments before I just caught the name, for his English, always quaint and beautiful, was at times a little halting; but when he said by way of explanation, "You know big fighter, Frenchman. The English they beat him in big battle," I grasped immediately of whom he spoke.

"What do you know of him?" I asked.

His voice lowered, almost as if he spoke a state secret. "I know how it is that English they beat him."

I have read many historians on this event, but to hear the Squamish version was a novel and absorbing thing. "Yes?" I said—my usual "leading" word to lure him into channels of tradition.

"Yes," he affirmed. Then, still in a half-whisper, he proceeded to tell me that it all happened through the agency of a single joint from the vertebra of a sea-serpent.

In telling me the story of Brockton Point and the valiant boy who killed the monster, he dwelt lightly on the fact that all people who approach the vicinity of the creature are palsied, both mentally and physically—bewitched, in fact—so that their bones become disjointed and their brains incapable; but today he elaborated upon this peculiarity until I harked back to the boy of Brockton Point and asked how it was that his body and brain escaped this affliction.

"He was all good, and had no greed," he replied. "He proof against all bad things."

I nodded understandingly, and he proceeded to tell me that all successful Indian fighters and warriors carried somewhere about their person a joint of a sea-serpent's vertebra, that the medicine men threw "the power" about them so that they were not personally affected by this little "charm," but that immediately they ap-

143

proached an enemy the "charm" worked disaster, and victory was assured to the fortunate possessor of the talisman. There was one particularly effective joint that had been treasured and carried by the warriors of a great Squamish family for a century. These warriors had conquered every foe they encountered, until the talisman had become so renowned that the totem pole of their entire "clan" was remodelled, and the new one crested by the figure of a single joint of a sea-serpent's vertebra.

About this time stories of Napoleon's first great achievements drifted across the seas; not across the land—and just here may be a clue to buried Coast-Indian history, which those who are cleverer at research than I, can puzzle over. The chief was most emphatic about the source of Indian knowledge of Napoleon.

"I suppose you heard of him from Quebec, through, perhaps, some of the French priests," I remarked.

"No, no," he contradicted hurriedly. "Not from East; we hear it from over the Pacific, from the place they call Russia." But who conveyed the news or by what means it came he could not further enlighten me. But a strange thing happened to the Squamish family about this time. There was a large blood connection, but the only male member living was a very old warrior, the hero of many battles, and the possessor of the talisman. On his death-bed his women of three generations gathered about him; his wife, his sisters, his daughters, his granddaughters, but not one man, nor yet a boy of his own blood stood by to speed his departing warrior spirit to the land of peace and plenty.

"The charm cannot rest in the hands of women," he murmured almost with his last breath. "Women may not war and fight other nations or other tribes; women are for the peaceful lodge and for the leading of little children. They are for holding baby hands, teaching baby feet to walk. No, the charm cannot rest with you, women. I have no brother, no cousin, no son, no grandson, and the charm must not go to a lesser warrior than I. None of our tribe, nor of any tribe on the coast, ever conquered me. The charm must go to one as unconquerable as I have been. When I am dead send it across the great salt chuck, to the victorious 'Frenchman'; they call him Napoleon Bonaparte." They were his last words.

The older women wished to bury the charm with him, but the younger women, inspired with the spirit of their generation, were determined to send it over seas. "In the grave it will be dead," they argued. "Let it still live on. Let it help some other fighter to greatness and victory."

As if to confirm their decision, the next day a small sealing vessel anchored in the Inlet. All the men aboard spoke Russian, save two thin, dark, agile sailors, who kept aloof from the crew and conversed in another language. These two came ashore with part of the crew and talked in French with a wandering Hudson's Bay trapper, who often lodged with the Squamish people. Thus the women, who yet mourned over their dead warrior, knew these two strangers to be from the land where the great "Frenchman" was fighting against the world.

Here I interrupted the chief. "How came the Frenchmen in a Russian sealer?" I asked.

"Captives," he replied. "Almost slaves, and hated by their captors, as the majority always hate the few." So the women drew those two Frenchmen apart from the rest and told them the story of the bone of the sea-serpent, urging them to carry it back to their own country and give it to the great "Frenchman" who was as courageous and as brave as their dead leader.

The Frenchmen hesitated; the talisman might affect them, they said; might jangle their own brains, so that on their return to Russia they would not have the sagacity to plan an escape to their own country; might disjoint their bodies, so that their feet and hands would be useless, and they would become as weak as children. But the women assured them that the charm only worked its magical powers over a man's enemies, that the ancient medicine man had "bewitched" it with this quality. So the Frenchmen took it and promised that if it were in the power of man they would convey it to "the Emperor."

As the crew boarded the sealer, the women watching from the shore observed strange contortions seize many of the men; some fell on the deck; some crouched, shaking as with palsy; some writhed for a moment, then fell limp and seemingly boneless; only the two Frenchmen stood erect and strong and vital—the Squamish talisman had already overcome their foes. As the little sealer set sail up the gulf she was commanded by a crew of two Frenchmen—men who had entered these waters as captives, who were leaving them as conquerors. The palsied Russians were worse than useless, and what became of them the chief could not state; presumably they were flung overboard, and by some trick of a kindly fate the Frenchmen at last reached the coast of France.

Tradition is so indefinite about their movements subsequent to sailing out of the Inlet, that even the ever-romantic and vividly coloured imaginations of the Squamish people have never supplied the details of this beautifully childish, yet strangely historical fairy tale. But the voices of the trumpets of war, the beat of drums throughout Europe heralded back to the wilds of the Pacific Coast forests the intelligence that the great Squamish "charm" eventually reached the person of Napoleon; that from this time onward his career was one vast victory, that he won battle after battle, conquered nation after nation, and but for the direst calamity that could befall a warrior would eventually have been master of the world.

"What was this calamity, Chief?" I asked, amazed at his knowledge of the great historical soldier and strategist.

The chief's voice again lowered to a whisper —his face was almost rigid with intentness as he replied:

"He lost the Squamish charm—lost it just before one great fight with the English people."

I looked at him curiously; he had been telling me the oddest mixture of history and superstition, of intelligence and ignorance, the most whimsically absurd, yet impressive, tale I ever heard from Indian lips.

"What was the name of the great fight—did you ever hear it?" I asked, wondering how

148

much he knew of events which took place at the other side of the world a century agone.

"Yes," he said, carefully, thoughtfully; "I hear the name sometime in London when I there. Railroad station there—same name."

"Was it Waterloo?" I asked.

He nodded quickly, without a shadow of hesitation. "That the one," he replied; "that's it, Waterloo."

The Lure in Stanley Park

There is a well-known trail in Stanley Park that leads to what I always love to call the "Cathedral Trees"—that group of some half-dozen forest giants that arch overhead with such superb loftiness. But in all the world there is no cathedral whose marble or onyx columns can vie with those straight, clean, brown tree-boles that teem with the sap and blood of life. There is no fresco that can rival the delicacy of lacework they have festooned between you and the

151

far skies. No tiles, no mosaic or inlaid marbles, are as fascinating as the bare, russet, fragrant floor outspreading about their feet. They are the acme of Nature's architecture, and in building them she has outrivalled all her erstwhile conceptions. She will never originate a more faultless design, never erect a more perfect edifice. But the divinely moulded trees and the man-made cathedral have one exquisite characteristic in common. It is the atmosphere of holiness. Most of us have better impulses after viewing a stately cathedral, and none of us can stand amid that majestic forest group without experiencing some elevating thoughts, some refinement of our coarser nature. Perhaps those who read this little legend will never again look at those cathedral trees without thinking of the glorious souls they contain, for according to the Coast Indians they do harbour human souls, and the world is better because they once had the speech and the hearts of mighty men.

My tillicum did not use the word "lure" in telling me this legend. There is no equivalent for the word in the Chinook tongue, but the gestures of his voiceful hands so expressed the quality of something between magnetism and charm that I have selected this word "lure" as best fitting what he wished to convey. Some few yards beyond the cathedral trees, an overgrown disused trail turns into the dense wilderness to the right. Only Indian eyes could discern that trail, and the Indians do not willingly go to that part of the park to the right of the great group. Nothing in this, nor yet the next world would tempt a Coast Indian into the compact centres of the wild portions of the park, for therein, concealed cunningly, is the "lure" they all believe in. There is not a tribe in the entire district that does not know of this strange legend. You will hear the tale from those that gather at Eagle Harbour for the fishing, from the Fraser River tribes, from the Squamish at the Narrows, from the Mission, from up the Inlet, even from the tribes at North Bend, but no one will volunteer to be your guide, for having once come within the "aura" of the lure it is a human impossibility to leave it. Your will-power is dwarfed, your intelligence blighted, your feet will refuse to lead you out by a straight trail, you will circle, circle for evermore about this magnet, for if death kindly comes to your aid, your immortal spirit will go on in that endless circling that will bar it from entering the Happy Hunting Grounds.

And, like the cathedral trees, the lure once lived, a human soul, but in this instance it was a soul depraved, not sanctified. The Indian belief is very beautiful concerning the results of good and evil in the human body. The Sagalie Tyee (God) has His own way of immortalizing each. People who are wilfully evil, who have no kindness in their hearts, who are bloodthirsty, cruel, vengeful, unsympathetic, the Sagalie Tyee turns to solid stone that will harbour no growth, even that of moss or lichen, for these stones contain no moisture, just as their wicked hearts lacked the milk of human kindness. The one famed exception, wherein a good man was transformed into stone, was in the instance of Siwash Rock, but as the Indian tells you of it he smiles with gratification as he calls your attention to the tiny tree cresting that imperial monument. He says the tree was always there to show the nations that the good in this man's heart kept on growing even when his body had ceased to be. On the other hand the Sagalie Tyee transforms the kindly people, the humane, sympathetic, charitable, loving people into trees, so that after death they may go on forever benefiting all mankind; they may yield fruit, give shade and shelter, afford unending service to the living, by their usefulness as building material and as firewood. Their saps and gums, their fibres, their leaves, their blossoms, enrich, nourish and sustain the human form; no evil is produced by trees—all, all is goodness, is hearty, is helpfulness and growth. They give

154

refuge to the birds, they give music to the winds, and from them are carved the bows and arrows, the canoes and paddles, bowls, spoons, and baskets. Their service to mankind is priceless; the Indian that tells you this tale will enumerate all these attributes and virtues of the trees. No wonder the Sagalie Tyee chose them to be the abode of souls good and great.

But the lure in Stanley Park is that most dreaded of all things, an evil soul. It is embodied in a bare, white stone, which is shunned by moss and vine and lichen, but over which are splashed innumerable jet-black spots that have eaten into the surface like an acid.

This condemned soul once animated the body of a witch-woman, who went up and down the coast, over seas and far inland, casting her evil eye on innocent people, and bringing them untold evils and diseases. About her person she carried the renowned "Bad Medicine" that every Indian believes in—medicine that weakened the arm of the warrior in battle, that caused deformities, that poisoned minds and characters, that engendered madness, that bred plagues and epidemics; in short, that was the seed of every evil that could befall mankind. This witch-woman herself was immune from death; generations were born and grew to old age, and died, and other generations arose in their stead, but the witch-woman went about, her heart set against her kind; her acts were evil, her purposes wicked, she broke hearts and bodies and souls; she gloried in tears, and revelled in unhappiness, and sent them broadcast wherever she wandered. And in His high heaven the Sagalie Tyee wept with sorrow for his afflicted human children. He dared not let her die, for her spirit would still go on with its evil doing. In mighty anger He gave command to His Four Men (always representing the Deity) that they should turn this witch-woman into a stone and enchain her spirit in its centre, that the curse of her might be lifted from the unhappy race.

So the Four Men entered their giant canoe, and headed, as was their custom, up the Narrows. As they neared what is now known as Prospect Point they heard from the heights above them a laugh, and looking up they beheld the witch-woman jeering defiantly at them. They landed and, scaling the rocks, pursued her as she danced away, eluding them like a will-o'-the-wisp as she called out to them sneeringly:

"Care for yourselves, O men of the Sagalie Tyee, or I shall blight you with my evil eye. Care for yourselves and do not follow me." On and on she danced through the thickest of the wilderness, on and on they followed until they reached the very heart of the seagirt neck of land we know as Stanley Park. Then the tallest, the mightiest of the Four Men, lifted his hand and cried out: "O woman of the stony heart, be stone for evermore, and bear forever a black stain for each one of your evil deeds." And as he spoke the witch-woman was transformed into this stone that tradition says is in the centre of the park.

Such is the legend of the Lure. Whether or not this stone is really in existence—who knows? One thing is positive, however, no Indian will ever help to discover it.

Three different Indians have told me that fifteen or eighteen years ago two tourists—a man and a woman—were lost in Stanley Park. When found a week later, the man was dead, the woman mad, and each of my informants firmly believed they had, in their wanderings, encountered "the stone" and were compelled to circle around it, because of its powerful lure.

But this wild tale fortunately has a most beautiful conclusion. The Four Men, fearing that the evil heart imprisoned in the stone would still work destruction, said: "At the end of the trail we must place so good and great a thing that it will be mightier, stronger, more powerful than this evil." So they chose from the nations the kindliest, most benevolent men,

men whose hearts were filled with the love of their fellow-beings, and transformed these merciful souls into the stately group of "Cathedral Trees."

How well the purpose of the Sagalie Tyee has wrought its effect through time! The good has predominated as He planned it to, for is not the stone hidden in some unknown part of the park where eyes do not see it and feet do not follow —and do not the thousands who come to us from the uttermost parts of the world seek that wondrous beauty spot, and stand awed by the majestic silence, the almost holiness of that group of giants?

More than any other legend that the Indians about Vancouver have told me does this tale reveal the love of the Coast native for kindness, and his hatred of cruelty. If these tribes really have ever been a warlike race I cannot think they pride themselves much on the occupation. If you talk with any of them and they mention some man they particularly like or admire, their first qualification of him is: "He's a kind man." They never say he is brave, or rich, or successful, or even strong, that characteristic so loved by the red man. To these Coast tribes if a man is "kind" he is everything. And almost without exception their legends deal with rewards for tenderness and self-abnegation, and personal and mental cleanliness.

Call them fairy tales if you wish to, they all have a reasonableness that must have originated in some mighty mind, and better than that, they all tell of the Indian's faith in the survival of the best impulses of the human heart, and the ultimate extinction of the worst.

In talking with my many good tillicums, I find this witch-woman legend is the most universally known and thoroughly believed in of all traditions they have honoured me by revealing to me.

Deer Lake

Few white men ventured inland, a century ago, in the days of the first Chief Capilano, when the spoils of the mighty Fraser River poured into copper-coloured hands, but did not find their way to the remotest corners of the earth, as in our times, when the gold from its sources, the salmon from its mouth, the timber from its shores are world-known riches.

The fisherman's craft, the hunter's cunning were plied where now cities and industries, trade and commerce, buying and selling hold sway. In those days the moccasined foot awoke no echo in the forest trails. Primitive weapons, arms, implements, and utensils were the only means of the Indians' food-getting. His livelihood depended upon his own personal prowess, his skill in woodcraft and water lore. And, as this is a story of an elk-bone spear, the reader must first be in sympathy with the fact that this rude instrument, most deftly fashioned, was of priceless value to the first Capilano, to whom it had come through three generations of ancestors all of whom had been experienced hunters and dexterous fishermen.

Capilano himself was without a rival as a spearsman. He knew the moods of the Fraser River, the habits of its thronging tenants, as no other man has ever known them before or since. He knew every isle and inlet along the coast, every boulder, the sand-bars, the still pools, the temper of the tides. He knew the spawning grounds, the secret streams that fed the larger rivers, the outlets of rock-bound lakes, the turns and tricks of swirling rapids. He knew the haunts of bird and beast and fish and fowl, and was master of the arts and artifice that man must use when matching his brain against the eluding wiles of the untamed creatures of the wilderness.

Once only did his cunning fail him, once only

did Nature baffle him with her mysterious fabric of waterways and land lures. It was when he was led to the mouth of the unknown river, which has evaded discovery through all the centuries, but which—so say the Indians— still sings on its way through some buried channel that leads from the lake to the sea.

He had been sealing along the shores of what is now known as Point Grey. His canoe had gradually crept inland, skirting up the coast to the mouth of False Creek. Here he encountered a very king of seals, a colossal creature that gladdened the hunter's eyes as game worthy of his skill. For this particular prize he would cast the elk-bone spear. It had never failed his sire, his grandsire, his great-grandsire. He knew it would not fail him now. A long, pliable, cedar-fibre rope lay in his canoe. Many expert fingers had woven and plaited that rope, had beaten and oiled it until it was soft and flexible as a serpent. This he attached to the spearhead, and with deft, unerring aim cast it at the king seal. The weapon struck home. The gigantic creature shuddered and, with a cry like a hurt child, it plunged down into the sea. With the rapidity and strength of a giant fish it scudded inland with the rising tide, while Capilano paid out the rope its entire length and, as it stretched taut, felt the canoe leap forwards, propelled by the mighty strength of the creature which lashed the waters into whirlpools, as though it was possessed with the power and properties of a whale.

Up the stretch of False Creek the man and monster drove their course, where a century hence great city bridges were to over-arch the waters. They strove and struggled each for the mastery, neither of them weakened, neither of them faltered—the one dragging, the other driving. In the end it was to be a matching of brute and human wits, not forces. As they neared the point where now Main Street bridge flings its shadow across the waters, the brute leaped high into the air, then plunged headlong into the depths. The impact ripped the rope from Capilano's hands. It rattled across the gunwhale. He stood staring at the spot where it had disappeared—the brute had been victorious. At low tide the Indian made search. No trace of his game, of his precious elk-bone spear, of his cedar-fibre rope, could be found. With the loss of the latter he firmly believed his luck as a hunter would be gone. So he patrolled the mouth of False Creek for many moons. His graceful, high-bowed canoe rarely touched other waters, but the seal king had disappeared. Often he thought long strands of drifting sea grasses were his lost cedar-fibre rope. With other spears, with other cedar fibres, with paddle-blade and cunning traps he dislodged the weeds from their moorings, but they slipped their slimy lengths through his eager hands : his best spear with its attendant coil was gone.

The following year he was sealing again off the coast of Point Grey, and one night after sunset he observed the red reflection from the west, which seemed to transfer itself to the eastern skies. Far into the night dashes of flaming scarlet pulsed far beyond the head of False Creek. The colour rose and fell like a beckoning hand and, Indian-like, he immediately attached some portentous meaning to the unusual sight. That it was some omen he never doubted, so he paddled inland, beached his canoe, and took the trail towards the little group of lakes that crowd themselves into the area that lies between the present cities of Vancouver and New Westminster. But long before he reached the shores of Deer Lake he discovered that the beckoning hand was in reality flame. The little body of water was surrounded by forest fires. One avenue alone stood open. It was a group of giant trees that as yet the flames had not reached. As he neared the point he saw a great moving mass of living things leaving the lake and hurrying northward through this one egress. He stood, listening, intently watching with alert eyes; the swirr of myriads of little travelling feet caught his quick ear—the moving mass was an immense colony of beavers. Thousands upon thousands of them. Scores of baby beavers staggered along, following their mothers; scores of older beavers that had felled trees and built dams through many seasons; a countless army of trekking fur bearers, all under the generalship of a wise old leader who, as king of the colony, advanced some few yards ahead of his battalions. Out of the waters through the forest towards the country to the north they journeyed. Wandering hunters said they saw them cross Burrard Inlet at the Second Narrows, heading inland as they reached the farther shore. But where that mighty army of royal little Canadians set up their new colony, no man knows. Not even the astuteness of the first Capilano ever discovered their destination. Only one thing was certain, Deer Lake knew them no more.

After their passing, the Indian retraced their trail to the water's edge. In the red glare of the encircling fires he saw what he at first thought was some dead and dethroned king beaver on the shore. A huge carcass lay half-in, half-out of the lake. Approaching it he saw the wasted body of a giant seal. There could never be two seals of that marvellous size. His intuition now grasped the meaning of the omen of the beckoning flame that had called him from the far coasts of Point Grey. He stooped above his dead conqueror and found, embedded in its decaying flesh, the elk-bone spear of his forefathers, and trailing away at the water's rim was a long flexible cedar-fibre rope.

As he extracted this treasured heirloom he felt the "power," that men of magic possess, creep up his sinewy arms. It entered his heart, his blood, his brain. For a long time he sat and chanted songs that only great medicine men may sing and, as the hours drifted by, the heat of the forest fires subsided, the flames diminished into smouldering blackness. At daybreak the forest fires were dead, but their beckoning fingers had served their purpose. The magic elk-bone spear had come back to its own.

Until the day of his death the first Capilano searched for the unknown river up which the seal travelled from False Creek to Deer Lake, but its channel is a secret that even Indian eyes have not seen.

But although those of the Squamish tribe tell and believe that the river still sings through its hidden trail that leads from Deer Lake to the sea, its course is as unknown, its channel is as hopelessly lost as the brave little army of beavers that a century ago marshalled their forces and travelled up into the great lone North.

A Royal Mohawk Chief

How many Canadians are aware that in Prince Arthur, Duke of Connaught, and only surviving son of Queen Victoria, who has been appointed to represent King George V in Canada, they undoubtedly have what many wish for—one bearing an ancient Canadian title as Governor-General of all the Dominion? It would be difficult to find a man more Canadian than any one of the fifty chiefs who compose the parliament of the ancient Iroquois nation, that loyal race of Redskins that has fought for the British crown against all of the enemies thereof, adhering to the British flag through the wars against both the French and the colonists.

Arthur, Duke of Connaught, is the only living white man who today has an undisputed right to the title of "Chief of the Six Nations Indians" (known collectively as the Iroquois). He possesses the privilege of sitting in their councils, of casting his vote on all matters relative to the governing of the tribes, the disposal of reservation lands, the appropriation of both the principal and interest of the more than half a million dollars these tribes hold in Government bonds at Ottawa, accumulated from the sales of their lands. In short, were every drop of blood in his royal veins red, instead of blue, he could not be more fully qualified as an Indian chief than he now is, not even were his title one of the fifty hereditary ones whose illustrious names composed the Iroquois confederacy before the Paleface ever set foot in America.

It was on the occasion of his first visit to Canada in 1869, when he was little more than a boy, that Prince Arthur received, upon his arrival at Quebec, an address of welcome from his Royal mother's "Indian Children" on the Grand River Reserve, in Brant county, Ontario. In addition to this welcome they had a request to make of him: would he accept the title of Chief and visit their reserve to give them the opportunity of conferring it?

One of the great secrets of England's success

with savage races has been her consideration, her respect, her almost reverence of native customs, ceremonies and potentates. She wishes her own customs and kings to be honoured, so she freely accords like honour to her subjects, it matters not whether they be white, black, or red.

Young Arthur was delighted—royal lads are pretty much like all other boys; the unique ceremony would be a break in the endless round of state receptions, banquets, and addresses. So he accepted the Red Indians' compliment, knowing well that it was the loftiest honour those people could confer upon a white man.

It was the morning of October first when the royal train steamed into the little city of Brantford, where carriages waited to take the Prince and his suite to the "Old Mohawk Church," in the vicinity of which the ceremony was to take place. As the Prince's especial escort, Onwanon-syshon, head chief of the Mohawks, rode on a jet-black pony beside the carriage. The chief was garmented in full native costume—a buckskin suit, beaded moccasins, headband of owl's and eagle's feathers, and ornaments hammered from coin silver that literally covered his coat and leggings. About his shoulders was flung a scarlet blanket, consisting of the identical broadcloth from which the British army tunics are made; this he "hunched" with his shoulders from time to time in true Indian fashion. As they drove along, the Prince chatted boyishly with his Mohawk escort, and once leaned forwards to pat the black pony on its shining neck and speak admiringly of it. It was a warm autumn day : the roads were dry and dusty and, after a mile or so, the boy-prince brought from beneath the carriage seat a basket of grapes. With his handkerchief he flicked the dust from them, handed a bunch to the chief and took one himself. An odd spectacle to be traversing a country road : an English prince and an Indian chief, riding amicably side-by-side, enjoying a banquet of grapes like two schoolboys.

On reaching the church, Arthur leapt lightly to the green-sward. For a moment he stood, rigid, gazing before him at his future brother-chiefs. His escort had given him a faint idea of what he was to see, but he certainly never expected to be completely surrounded by three hundred full-blooded Iroquois braves and warriors, such as now encircled him on every side. Every Indian was in war paint and feathers, some stripped to the waist, their copper-coloured skins brilliant with paints, dyes and "patterns"; all carried tomahawks, scalping-knives, and bows and arrows. Every red throat gave a tremendous war-whoop as he alighted, which was repeated again and again, as for that half moment he stood silent, a slim boyish figure, clad in light grey tweeds—a singlar contrast to the stalwarts in gorgeous costumes who crowded about him. His young face paled to ashy whiteness, then with true British grit he extended his right hand and raised his black "billy-cock" hat with his left. At the same time he took one step forwards. Then the war cries broke forth anew, deafening, savage, terrible cries, as one by one the entire three hundred filed past, the Prince shaking hands with each one, and removing his glove to do so. This strange reception over, Onwanonsyshon rode up and, flinging his scarlet blanket on the grass, dismounted, and asked the Prince to stand on it.

Then stepped forwards an ancient chief, father of Onwanonsyshon, and Speaker of the Council. He was old in inherited and personal loyalty to the British crown. He had fought under Sir Isaac Brock at Queenston Heights in 1812, while yet a mere boy, and upon him was laid the honour of making his Queen's son a chief. Taking Arthur by the hand this venerable warrior walked slowly to and fro across the blanket, chanting as he went the strange, wild formula of induction. From time to time he was interrupted by loud expressions of approval and assent from the vast throng of encircling braves, but apart from this no sound was heard but the low, weird monotone of a ritual older than the white man's footprints in North America.

It is necessary that a chief of each of the three "clans" of the Mohawks shall assist in this ceremony. The veteran chief, who sang the formula, was of the Bear clan. His son, Onwanonsyshon, was of the Wolf (the clanship descends through the mother's side of the family). Then one other chief, of the Turtle clan, and in whose veins coursed the blood of the historic Brant, now stepped to the edge of the scarlet blanket. The chant ended, these two young chiefs received the Prince into the Mohawk tribe, conferring upon him the name of "Kavakoudge," which means "the sun flying from East to West under the guidance of the Great Spirit."

Onwanonsyshon then took from his waist a brilliant deep-red sash, heavily embroidered with beads, porcupine quills and dyed moose hair, placing it over the Prince's left shoulder and knotting it beneath his right arm. The ceremony was ended. The Constitution that Hiawatha had founded centuries ago, a Constitution wherein fifty chiefs, no more, no less, should form the parliament of the "Six Nations," had been shattered and broken, because this race of loyal red men desired to do honour to a slender young boy-prince, who now bears the fifty-first title of the Iroquois.

Many white men have received from these same people honorary titles, but none has been bestowed through the ancient ritual, with the imperative members of the three clans assisting, save that borne by Arthur of Connaught.

After the ceremony the Prince entered the church to autograph his name in the ancient Bible which, with a silver Holy Communion service, a bell, two tablets inscribed with the Ten Commandments, and a bronze British coat-of-arms, had been presented to the Mohawks by Queen Anne. He inscribed "Arthur" just below the "Albert Edward" which, as Prince of Wales, the late king wrote when he visited Canada in 1860.

When he returned to England, Chief Kava-koudge sent his portrait, together with one of Queen Victoria and the Prince Consort, to be placed in the Council House of the "Six Nations," where they decorate the walls today.

As I write, I glance up to see, in a corner of my room, a draping scarlet blanket, made of British army broadcloth, for the chief who rode the jet-black pony so long ago was the writer's father. He was not here to wear it when Arthur of Connaught again set foot on Canadian shores.

Many of these facts I have culled from a

paper that lies on my desk; it is yellowing with age, and bears the date, "Toronto, October 2, 1869," and on the margin is written in a clear, half-boyish hand, "Onwanonsyshon, with kind regards from your brother-chief, Arthur."